Liberating Teaching
and Learning

Liberating Teaching and Learning

Turn it Upside Down, Watch African American Learners (All Learners) SOAR!

By

Dr. Bettye Chitman Haysbert

ISBN: 978-1-7334943-1-1 (paperback)

To:

My sisters, Alice Whitehurst (Big Sister), Eloise Gatson, Mc Johnny Pearson, the enduring spirit of Louise Hill, Clifford Winston, and Gloria Gates, and my son, Darryl. I give infinite love and gratitude to you.

My extended family and circle of friends. Thanks for the motivation, inspiration, and valuable feedback.

Representative Elijah Cummings, and those like him, who, despite many accomplishments, was and are wrongly placed in special education classes.

Parents who must fight racism, discrimination, and oppression everywhere, all the time, and still you rise— that's brilliance!

The young reader, anyone who can and wants to read this book, should read it—no age or grade requirement. You may not understand everything during the first read—keep reading!

Teachers and learners who are ready to restructure the classroom by working as partners to plan and teach together, ensuring all learners can SOAR!

Our lives begin to end the day we become silent about things that matter.
—Martin Luther King Jr.

I won't rest until black children are taught to love themselves as themselves.
—Frances Cress Welsing

TABLE OF CONTENTS

A Revolutionary Way to Teach and Learn

*The program for the uplift of the Negro in this country must
be based upon a scientific study of the Negro from within
to develop in him the power to do for himself what his
oppressors will never do to elevate him to the level of others.*
—Carter G. Woodson, 1933

We're embarking upon radical change in
education. I invite you to join the revolution in
this "classroom restructuring." In order to go with me in
this revolution, you must take the "lid" off your thinking.

Have you ever seen trained fleas in a jar? You don't need

a lid to keep them in. That's because when the trainer first puts them in the jar, he puts a lid on it, and the fleas jump up and down frantically hitting their heads against it. Finally, after a lot of headaches, they stop jumping and settle into their new situation. Now, when the lid is removed, the fleas are held captive by a mind-set of low expectations that says, "So high and no higher."

Imagine you going to school each day where your teachers know and respect you and are glad to see you. Teachers and your classmates can't wait to see what you are going to plan for your lessons that day, in what creative way you will present your lessons, and how you will help others complete theirs. Everybody is excited because you always bring your unique perspective to any situation.

You feel supported at this school because of your great teachers, who coplan and coteach with you and your team. Your teachers have done the hard work of unlearning racism and have gotten in touch with prejudices, racial biases, discriminatory and oppressive practices, and attitudes they had. They are ready to step aside and let your brilliance and intelligence shine while nurturing and motivating you to reach your full potential.

As soon as you enter the class, the teacher and your team members check in to see how you are doing and whether you are ready to learn because they know how important it is that you feel they care. The experiences, history, and culture of people of color are used to teach each day (music always plays), and you are supported by a fantastic learning team. You meet not only to help each other to accomplish academic tasks but to listen to and resolve personal problems members may be having.

You and other people of color choose class projects that empower you and your communities, addressing issues of racism, discrimination, and oppression to solve social justice issues and anything else of importance to you. Because everyone is engaged in meaningful learning, your learning style, behavioral styles, and culture are known and appreciated; there is little to no issue of "behavior problems." The only occasional behavior problem comes from European American learners who are disoriented from the shift—everything is upside down. Their history, culture, experiences, learning styles, and perspectives are no longer the center of all learning.

African Americans are among the highest achievers, especially in math and science, reclaiming your unknown and forgotten history of excellence in math, science, and technology. Therefore, you are not found in the few special education classes in the school districts. You are setting educational trends just as you do in sports, music, and anywhere else you are free to be yourself. "What is this?" "Where is this?"

Well, hang on to your boots, because you're about to learn a "Revolutionary" way to teach and learn—radical classroom restructuring that will free you to be yourself and achieve in ways like never before! Let's go make it happen! There is an African Proverb that says,

When spider webs unite, they can tie up a lion.

African Proverb

I am an African American (AA) woman who received her education in a segregated school setting in the South that provided strong affective support. It was a school setting where the school community expected that we students would excel, and we soared. Our cultural needs were supported, so our brilliance and intelligence shone! Our teachers and administrators lived in our community, knew our parents, and held the same regard and expectations for us as did our parents.

They taught us our history, and we felt a sense of pride for who we were.

Upon coming to San Francisco to begin my teaching career, I was alarmed at the number of African American students who were placed into special education classes and labeled "Educable Mentally Handicapped." This was my introduction to special education. In my classes in the South, learners who didn't learn as fast as we did stayed in that grade, without judgment, until they learned what they were supposed to learn.

I taught for several years in special education classes and quickly realized that the students' failure was directly related to the failure of the school system to educate them. The majority of the learners in my classes and learners in my friends' classes simply did not have the knowledge or skills to be successful in the regular classroom. These learners were given a couple of tests (which are still in use over forty years later) that required them to exhibit academic skills they did not have. So, they were labeled and placed into special education classes, forever.

At that time, I vowed to prove that it was not the learners that had a problem; rather, it was the school system with the problem. This critical realization and my quest to promote understandings in this area served as the impetus for participating in various school reform efforts, undertaking my doctoral study, which looked at the practices of teachers who were effective in teaching AA learners, the creation of an innovative way to teach struggling readers quickly, and finally, a book for teachers and learners. All done in the interest of proving that it is the educational system which is the problem, not the learners.

INTRODUCTION

What Is This Book About?

R ead this book and unlock the brilliance, intelligence, creativity, resourcefulness, strength, and spontaneity of AA and all learners. Watch them *SOAR!*

I know many of you teachers and learners have been waiting for this. Here it is!

A simple step-by-step self-empowering guide for teachers and learners to help each other radically restructure teaching and learning in the classroom. Unmotivated, unchallenged potential dropouts become motivated, engaged high achievers, quickly. Teachers are freed from trying to be everything to everybody. You step back and allow learners to come forward and become more responsible for their learning. Learners are liberated by being given a choice in what and how they learn. You know our schools are not working optimally for all learners. They embrace some and push others out.

In this conversational and action-oriented guide, you are shown how you two can radically restructure the classroom together, with no extra money and no additional materials, just a willingness to coplan, teach, learn from each other, and use the history, culture, interests, strengths, and experiences of people of color in all lessons. Then watch that classroom transform.

This kind of learning represents a paradigm shift in how we teach and learn. A shift from a European American (EA) curriculum and instruction to an inclusive one that benefits all learners because their experiences, history, and culture are used each day as the basis for learning.

AAs are the focus, because when we use what works for them, it works for everybody, but it doesn't work the other way around. Also, AAs have led all civil rights and major social justice changes in America, and all people have benefited. Finally, AA learners are punished the most severely in the education system, often for being different.

So, when African American students:

- are in caring classrooms,
- learn their history and culture,
- are free to explore their interests,
- use their strengths to learn,
- use their experiences as the basis for curriculum, and
- are free to solve real problems important to them,

motivation and achievement increase, and they *SOAR!*

When African American students SOAR!, so do all learners, but it doesn't work the other way around!

Why Write It?

- To share a quick way to bring **big** change to our classrooms.
- To tell you that nothing is wrong with you—the educational system is not made for you; we have to change it.
- To tell you that you are brilliant, intelligent, creative, and resourceful—but are not given opportunities, in the classroom, to show who you are, show how you learn, and follow your interests.

- ◆ To lighten the teaching load for teachers.
- ◆ To help teachers understand that you have potentially twenty-five to thirty partners in the classroom each day who are able to coplan and teach the lessons.
- ◆ To introduce a dual strategy, combining liberating teaching and learning (LTL) and cooperative learning (CL) approaches which have been proven to provide many benefits for all students, especially AAs and Latinos.

CRISIS IN EDUCATION FOR AFRICAN AMERICAN STUDENTS

It was well understood that if by teaching of his history the White man could be further assured of his superiority and the Negro could be made to feel that he had always been a failure and that the subjection of his will to some other race is necessary. The freedman, then, would still be a slave.

—Carter G. Woodson, 1933

What Is It?

You are brilliant and intelligent learners but are not given opportunities to SOAR! in school the way schools are presently structured. You are not free to be yourselves, learn your history and culture, explore your interests, show how you learn best, and solve real-life problems that make your lives and communities better. Because schools are not set up to support you, many of you struggle to do well, and when you don't succeed, you are punished, and low expectations are continued for your classroom performance. Because of these factors, many of you become less interested and motivated to learn. In order to succeed, you must try to fit (deny yourself) into a school structure that was designed for and by EAs. It teaches you nothing positive about your history and culture, only about EAs; still we want you to be excited to go to school every day to hear about someone else.

No wonder you are the most disciplined, suspended, expelled, placed in special education classes, with the lowest expectations and often the lowest achievers. The list goes on. In fact, for many, research shows that as you move upward in grades your reading moves downward. All of this must change.

This Is What We Know

- ◆ Outside of the classroom, you SOAR!/shine in sports, music, and various forms of performance. However, you are not allowed to bring those skills and knowledge inside the classroom.
- ◆ You SOAR! when you are allowed to express who you are, engage in your interests, and have your experiences be part of the curriculum.

- ◆ There has been a shortage of teachers for decades, and because of the need to have a warm body in the classroom, we have:
  - ➢ some unqualified teachers, and
  - ➢ some teachers who would rather not be there, and especially with certain learners.

Many positive reform efforts have taken place across the country, and too many of you are still not achieving to the extent that you can. EA history, culture, and experiences remain center in those reforms, whereas LTL moves EAs out of the center of learning and puts them in line with all other ethnic groups. LTL also includes learners in this reform.

What's Causing It?

Institutional Racism and Cultural Mismatch

Our educational system was designed by, and for, European American men. For years, schools served only White males. Later, a few White females were admitted.

The curricula focused on European American history, culture, perspective, experiences, and interests. Schools were established to promote EAs and ensure their success by making claims about who they are and what they have achieved. Then they required everybody to go through their schools being taught the same curriculum in the same way—whether it supported you or your needs or not. Everybody else leaves those schools thinking no other ethnic group contributes, or ever contributed, in positive ways to this country or the world. This is one of the many lies we tell and is a form of racism—when one so-called race claims superiority over another and has the power to legalize it. At the same time, the behavior is oppressive as well.

Schools propagated the notion that White people were smart, knew it all, and made all the history in the world and that no one else did anything of significance. That lie is still being perpetuated.

Their instructional method of lecturing, from England, that fits their learning style best is still being used today. The lecturing method:

◆ is one person, a teacher, who knows it all and controls what and how learners learn and punishes those who don't—that's a form of oppression, control;
◆ is controlling—it tells you what and how to think, all through the worldview of EAs;
◆ is indoctrinating and oppressive—it gives only one perspective and the belief that this way of learning and curriculum is superior to others, if there was anything worth learning from others;

- is a classroom where all learners sit quietly in rows and speak only when told to;
- uses mainly teacher talk (teacher sits or stands in the front of the room);
- only uses paper, pencil, textbook, worksheets, and workbooks to learn;
- thinks you are smart only if you can read, write, and do math the way EAs do; and
- maintains strict control.

EAs, especially White men, who were the first benefactors of education in the United States, continue to receive the most benefits from what is taught and how it's taught.

Seventeenth-century classroom structure and behavior—
this is the way classrooms looked in the 1600s.

This form of teaching and learning teaches people of color how to be imitators of White people and value European American history and culture over their own culture (way of being), contributing to low self-image for many people of color. Because EAs promote themselves as superior to others through what we teach and how we teach in our schools, and because **every** citizen goes through our schools and receives the same indoctrination, our educational system is the greatest perpetuator of racism and oppression in our society—hence the institutional racism.

This is how Elizabeth Martinez Smith explains it in her article "Racism: It Is Always There":

"One does not have to exercise a choice to perpetuate a racist act. The organization's rules, procedures, curriculum and instruction have already pre-structured the choices against people of color. An individual only has to conform to the operating norms and value of the organization and it will do the discriminating for him or her."

So, all of us who maintain the status quo adhere to traditional standards, perpetuate an unjust system, and we could say, discriminate against ourselves. Hmmm.

Our citizens exit our schools ready to perpetuate the values, norms, and established order of this society.
The EA lecture model is still being used in schools today, and many classrooms still arrange desks in rows. This model pushes out others whose history, culture, and interests are different from European Americans'. Most people learn best the way learning naturally takes place, experientially, often in groups, and through interactions.

Now, while you are moving through our schools, the farther you are away from how European Americans look, speak, behave, and learn, the more you are labeled "deviant" or "deficient," at which time you will be removed from the mainstream and placed in programs or institutions just for being you. So, as you emerge from this form of education, you must be careful not to be little White people in dark skin.

"The Animal School", by George Reavis

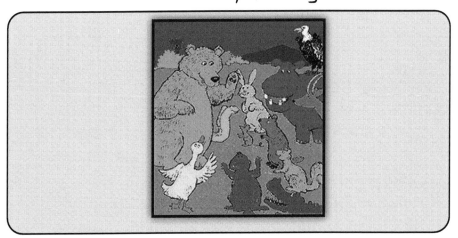

Once upon a time the animals decided they must do something heroic to meet the problems of a "new world," so they organized a school. They had adopted an activity curriculum consisting of running, climbing, swimming, and flying. To make it easier to administer the curriculum, all the animals took all the subjects.

The duck was excellent in swimming. In fact, better than his instructor. But he made only passing grades in flying and was very poor in running. Since he was slow in running, he had to stay after school and also drop swimming in order to practice running. This was kept up until his webbed feet were badly worn and he was only average in swimming. But average was acceptable in school, so nobody worried about that, except the duck.

The rabbit started at the top of the class in running but had a nervous breakdown because of so much makeup work in swimming.

The squirrel was excellent in climbing until he developed frustration in the flying class, where his teacher made him start from the ground up instead of the treetop down. He also developed a "charlie horse" from overexertion and then got a C in climbing and a D in running.

The eagle was a problem child and was disciplined severely. In the climbing class, he beat all the others to the top of the tree but insisted on using his own way to get there.

At the end of the year, an abnormal eel that could swim exceedingly well and also run, climb, and fly a little had the highest average and was valedictorian.

The prairie dogs stayed out of school and fought the tax levy because the administration would not add digging and burrowing to the curriculum. They apprenticed their children to a badger and later joined the groundhogs and gophers to start a successful private school.

What does this story/fable mean to you? Learners are uniquely different, and schools should plan learning experiences that support individual strengths, or we set learners up to fail. We must maximize our strengths, not handicap our potential by becoming good at something that isn't natural for us.

We, people, are different. Different does not mean deficient; in fact, different is good! Don't be afraid to be different. Embrace what your supreme maker gave you.

EAs have established themselves as the standard for how we should look, speak, and behave. EAs are the people who most benefit from the way schools exist today and those of color who can and desire to fit themselves into this mold.

Since the majority (80 percent) of teachers in our schools are of European descent, it becomes important to show the differences of each culture to better understand African American student needs, while eliminating the expectation that AA students will behave in the same manner as White students. When they do not, they should not be punished.

African American students generally share certain cultural characteristics that EAs do not. Many scholars have contributed to the body of knowledge/research which characterizes the African American culture as exhibiting a sense of:

- vitality—active, energy, strong;
- resilience—toughness, ability to bounce back from difficulties;
- physical interaction;
- oral communication;
- active learning;
- cooperative interdependence—in team learning, all depend on each other;
- spirituality;
- worldview—how you see the world and you in it.

Your Brilliance and Intelligence

Your brilliance and intelligence are not allowed to shine in the classroom the way you are free to shine outside of the classroom in areas where you are liberated to be who you are and use what's inside of you. I want you to know your time has come.

How to Fix It

By Radically Changing the Classroom and Using a Revolutionary Way to Teach and Learn called Liberating Teaching and Learning

> *To educate the Negro, we must find out exactly what his background is, what he is today, what his possibilities are, how to begin with him as he is and make him a better individual of the kind that he is. Instead of cramming the Negro's mind with what others have shown that they can do, we should develop his latent powers that he may perform in society a part of which others are not capable.*
> —Carter G. Woodson, 1933

I say let's be sure we are educating rather than training our learners. According to Dr. Frederick Haynes, to educate is to call out of you what is already there to be used for your benefit. To train, you train animals; you are trained to operate contrary to your character to benefit others—the trainers.

Turn Teaching and Learning Upside Down-How to Flip the Script

Education must begin with who the learner is
> —Carter G. Woodson, 1933

Learning is the active construction of meaning, not a passive receptive process.
> —Unknown

Move From the lecture method—(a way to control how you learn and what you learn, instruction and curriculum coming only from the teacher who is considered a controller/enforcer—aimed to indoctrinate), move from European history/culture and worldview, set up by White Men for White Men—desks in rows, and finally move from the use of workbooks, worksheets, and dull textbooks.

Move To Liberating Teaching and Learning, an interactive learning method to accommodate all people's history, culture, interests, worldview, and experiences, where the teacher is the facilitator/guide/consultant—colearner—and liberates learners to learn what they want and how they learn best. Then, teach that learning to peers. Learning increases exponentially, finally allowing learners' brilliance and intelligence to shine.

Schools are slowly noticing the new kind of learner emerging in our schools, but they are not stepping up to meet those needs. I realize some schools are doing better at educating some of our children, but change efforts have not produced needed change for people of color, because the basic EA structure and curriculum remain the same and allow EAs to maintain their advantage.

Instead, schools choose to label millions of you "disabled" and "behavior problems" and ignore your learning needs and potential.

Some of you are simply tired—so am I—of hearing the lies about European Americans and never being taught the truth about ourselves and others. This is a form of oppression (attempting to keep you ignorant) and racism (claiming their race is superior to others). African Americans, Latinos, and Native (First) Americans have been around longer than European Americans and have an extremely rich history and culture that we all could benefit from knowing.

We must liberate learning environments and trust you to create tailor-made experiences that meet your needs and interests. You will really begin to learn, maybe, for the first time because:

- Teachers don't know it all and can't do it all!
- The teacher is only ONE. S/he has twenty-five to thirty potential partners.
- Learners bring knowledge and experiences— they are not empty vessels.
- Coplanning and coteaching create a rich, dynamic classroom for teachers and learners.

Description

Liberating teaching and learning (LTL) requires a paradigm shift in the educational experience. LTL is an instructional strategy where teachers and learners share equally in creating and executing the learning experience. LTL incorporates educational philosophies which support a variety of researched teaching and learning models proven to be effective in increasing achievement for African American learners and others.

Pillars of Liberating Teaching and Learning Are Varied and Research Based

The pillars – LTL is:

- affective education—learners need to feel safe and cared for and feel that there is fairness and justice;

- learner centered—students have choice, learn their way, take on responsibility;
- focused on high expectations—it believes learners can learn anything;
- social justice- and action-oriented in the classroom, school, and world;
- based on relevant curriculum and instructional strategies—coplanned with learners and teacher;
- based on critical thinking through problem solving in real-world contexts to change students' lives and their circumstances;
- informed by constructivism and progressivism—the learner is the active constructor of meaning/understanding of knowledge;
- based on cooperative/collaborative learning—interactive team learning;
- a cultural form of learning, behaving, and communicating styles—culture influences the way we gather, analyze, process, and utilize information;
- a form of meta teaching and learning—*thinking* about how we teach and learn, and about what we do;
- a transformative form of learning—it changes understanding of self, fosters revision of belief system, and changes lifestyle;
- performance driven—self-reflection, self-expression, peer feedback, projects based in real world contexts aimed to change their lives for the better.

Rationale

Teachers Don't Know It All and Can't Do It All!

What if teachers allowed learners to coplan and teach? When we teach, we learn! The more the teacher teaches, the more the teacher learns.

◆ The role of teachers is becoming increasingly complex and vast. Teachers are expected to know how to fulfill the emotional, social, and academic needs of learners from diverse backgrounds; know their interests, cultures, and personal concerns brought to the classroom; and then create and design all learning experiences to motivate all learners and address all behavioral challenges. Impossible!

Our classrooms are extremely diverse.

Students:

◆ come from different cultures,
◆ have different:
  ➤ learning styles and interests,
  ➤ levels of emotional and social maturity,
  ➤ language needs, and
  ➤ levels of academic readiness in various subjects.

Learners Bring Knowledge and Experiences—They are Not Empty Vessels

What if learners were allowed to dovetail their diverse knowledge, perspectives, and experiences with school knowledge?

Learners would feel valued and motivated. When we endeavor to educate vs. train our citizens, we want to bring out of them what is already there, in order to **empower** them, to change their lives and society.

How It Works

Teacher is Only One; She or He Has Twenty-Five to Thirty Potential Partners

What if learners and teachers worked together—coplanned *what* and *how* each learner learned his or her tasks?

- ◆ Teachers and learners negotiate the *what* (curriculum) and *how* (activity/instruction) of the learning experience, thereby creating relevant, interesting curriculum and instructional strategies which eliminate boredom.

Benefits

A Rich, Dynamic Classroom for *Teachers* and *Learners*

Teachers

- Teachers are learners; learners are teachers.
- Teachers coplan and teach with learners—they free learners to plan and meet their own diverse learning needs and interests.
- A lighter planning and teaching load relieves the pressure on teachers to try to be everything to everybody.
- Learners show teachers who they are and what they need.
- It is important to allow more choice in **what** and **how** learners learn—more learner responsibility and accountability.
- Less effort is needed to motivate learners—students will be more self-motivated.
- Automatic integrated and multicultural education ensures curriculum relevancy.
- Students gain broad and deep knowledge.
- In-class professional development occurs.
- Teachers learn diverse instructional strategies—multiple approaches to learning and expressing understanding that are effortlessly unique to your learners.

- All participants learn the history, culture, interests, and various intelligences of learners from each other.
- Classrooms experience less discipline issues—learners have more buy-in/engagement.
- Entire classes are enriched—more relevant teaching and learning.
- Teachers learn the student's preferred style of learning.
- Lessons are automatically individualized and differentiated.
- The teacher's view of learners changes; thus, expectations change. Expectations are less likely to change for learners if the teacher never sees different behavior or achievement.

Learners learn to:

- see themselves as capable independent and life-long learners,
- feel valued and supported,
- work as a team,
- understand how:
  - to learn,
  - they learn,
  - to teach others to learn while teaching the teacher how students learn.

This leads to increased:

◆ achievement,
◆ motivation,
◆ self-esteem and empowerment,
◆ retention,
◆ knowledge—broad and deep,
◆ vocabulary, and
◆ comprehension.

Learners further learn to:

◆ coplan and teach with teacher and peers,
◆ utilize their strengths and interests and study their history and culture ("learn it their way"),
◆ activate prior knowledge and bridge to present,
◆ differentiate instruction and assignments, optimizing learning,
◆ become independent, self-directed, and thriving citizens in society.

When the student is learner and teacher, teaching what s/he learns to others, s/he is more motivated and engaged, and teacher and student learning expand exponentially.

This simple technique is powerful and far reaching. It can be used in all subject areas, with all learners. With each assignment, give choice.

Outside Brilliance and Intelligence

Again, your time has come. You can begin to bring about positive change and achievement in the classroom by using LTL, which offers benefits in many areas:

- Advocating for choice in what you learn and how to learn it. Learning your history and culture and using them to help you to learn other things. This shifts us away from EA-centered curriculum and instruction.
- Coplanning and coteaching with your teacher. Learn both new curriculum and instructional strategies.
- Use cooperative learning to increase learning fast and support your peers. You'll learn more.

All of these help the teacher!

Map showing where our
culture influences others

Beautiful, brilliant, and intelligent ones, your culture is lauded outside of our classrooms, throughout the United States, and around the world. Many people around the world embrace our explicit culture (we'll talk about this later). *We are trendsetters.*

They admire and imitate your culture:

◆ Music. Played all over the world. I escorted some high school children to Russia, and as we walked down the streets of Kiev, there, displayed in a large window of a shop, was a picture of a beautiful album by Whitney Houston.

◆ Dance. Rhythm-entertainment (singing, dancing). It is common to arrive in an international city and as soon as you are recognized as an African American, for the natives to call out their favorite singers/artists as a way to connect and let you know they know and like someone from your ethnic group.

- Performing Arts. Movies, plays. Let's just take a look at the recent *Black Panther* movie: a thirty-three-year-old former football player, Ryan Coogler, director and writer. This movie was a hit worldwide. EAs tell us no one wants to see our movies internationally—far from being true. Please understand people say this to deter you.
- Sports. What can you say about sports except that AAs dominate and their brilliance and intelligence shine because players are free to use their strengths and uniquenesses in their areas of interests?
- Literature. Maya Angelou, Marley Dias, Alice Walker ... we could go on with this list.
- Use of language. The poetic speech rhythms— rapping, voice inflections, use of inventive words, etc.
- Your style. The manner in which you present and display your uniqueness (your walk, your clothes, your hair).
- Hair. So unique. First, it grows out from our heads rather than down (embrace that) in many textures. It is hard for anyone to show the diversity of our hair styles—there is no limit, from naturals, braids, twists, locks, waves, plaits, fades, and afros to straight.
- While teaching a class in Kuwait, I was invited to have a meal with a family who had a teenage boy who came into the house with pants sagging (would rather have some other aspect of our culture copied), and he was listening to AA hip-hop/rap.

- Even how we fight for our freedom in the United States. I recall a cruise trip to South America. We had a cultural exchange, in Rio de Janeiro, where a professor came aboard the ship and spoke to us about their history and culture. The professor told us how the darker, African Brazilians used AA civil rights techniques of protests and other practices to fight for and win their civil rights.
- Leadership. We have incredible leaders.

Outside Brilliance and Intelligence Changed the Course of History

President Obama's Inauguration 2009

◆ Compassion. I'm sure you can think of many ways we show compassion—despite all the ways we have been killed and abused by EAs, we often follow with an expression of our humanity. Read the story of Anthony Ray Hinton, a brilliant man who, as a young man, was sentenced to death row for a crime that the EA arresting officers knew he didn't commit.

◆ You notice academics are not mentioned here, but that part of you must be expressed. Now. You are just as capable in academics as in sports or any other area in which you excel.

A Story from Abroad

I asked my nephew Bernard, who has traveled extensively to some very interesting places abroad, including having worked for almost two years in Colombia, South America, to share some stories. He has chosen to share a couple of experiences that he had in Colombia and China.

Here he makes a comparison between what happens to him in the United States and what happened while he was traveling in Colombia. First, he dispels the myth that people in other countries don't like African Americans. In fact, he says, "I felt more like a human being"—an example:

I was walking in this rather upper-class community of Colombia and women were passing up and down the street by me, not the least bit concerned that they were walking past a Black man on the streets or feeling the need to be cautious. Then, I saw a little old woman approaching. I knew she would grab her purse or move to the side. No, she didn't. She didn't even look at me. That was such a liberating feeling. On the other hand, in the United States, in my community in Los Angeles, which is middle to upper class, even in the daylight, as I'm walking down the street, White women will grab their purses and move away as if they don't want to get too close.

Another incident I noticed that was pretty different from what happens in the United States. When we get on a public bus here in the United States, people will take all other empty seats before they take a seat next to an African American. They will take the seat next to you as the last resort. For me in Colombia, when I sat on the bus, no matter how many seats were vacant, people chose to come and sit next to me.

I was still working in Colombia when the movie *Black Panther* by Ryan Coogler was playing. All of my students loved it. Not one student didn't like it. They were not concerned that it had all Black characters. That was fine with them. Yet another myth dispelled that people abroad don't want to see our movies.

The last thing I'll mention about South America is that when I was in Peru, I toured a church that had a statue of the first Black saint in the Americas, St. Martin de Porres, often called the saint of charity because of all the work he did for the poor and sick. Also, a famous painting, *El Senor de los Milagros* (Christ of Miracles), painted by an enslaved African in Lima, has been the only surviving piece after two earthquakes. People carry a replica through the streets in one of the biggest processions in the world.

The other experiences were in small towns in China, Yangshuo and Guilin. I was fascinated with the number of young high school and college age people who asked if they could take a picture with me. Then, there was this older man who wanted to take a picture with me and his son. His wife took the picture. The older gentlemen was so happy to meet me and smiled and waved when I saw him in other areas of the Main Street in Yangshuo. That happened throughout my travels in China.

Further, our brilliance and intelligence shine when an eleven-year-old activist, Marley Diaz, becomes fed up with reading books about, in her words, "White boys and their dogs," and seeing no one who looked like her. So, she found books with Black heroines, and started collecting them and sharing them with other people who looked like her. She even sent them as far as Jamaica, home of her parents. That wasn't enough; she wrote her own book, *Marley Dias Gets It Done, and So Can You!* Marley is changing the face of children's literature.

I must mention the ladies in *Hidden Figures*, who helped put men on the Moon. The women were referred to as Human Computers (NASA's Black women mathematicians).

In 2006, Hassan Bennett, of Philadelphia, received a life sentence at age twenty-three for a crime he did not commit. After serving more than a decade in prison, and after doing away with an ineffective defense attorney, he represented himself in his own retrial. Even though he knew nothing about law; he learned. Bennett, now thirty-three years old, learned enough about the legal system in prison to represent himself and won his case. He is now free.

There are many more examples of how our brilliance and intelligence shine outside of the classroom. But we can and must liberate and restructure our classrooms so that your brilliance and intelligence will shine there also. That means classrooms must liberate you to be yourself, express your creativity, show who you are, learn your history, and embrace your culture.

Geniuses

Geniuses

Be inspired by some of our young geniuses— there are many more than those listed here. They are all fantastic. It was hard for me to choose. So, use the Internet and read more. Find people who look like you and are achievers to stay inspired. Check out the following:

Black Children: Natural Geniuses-(YouTube)

Twenty Black Child Prodigies Mainstream Media Doesn't Talk About—Read Their Stories. Where are they now?

Jaylen Bledsoe

Jaylen Bledsoe, fifteen, of Hazelwood, Missouri, started his own company, Bledsoe Technologies, at age thirteen. It is now worth around $3.5 million.

Rochelle Ballantyne

At seventeen, Rochelle Ballantyne is one of the top chess players in the world. This Brooklyn, New York, native is a high school senior now, but her name is still at the top of Intermediate School 318's list of best players. She is on the verge of becoming the first Black American female to earn the title of chess master.

Carson Huey-You

This eleven-year-old is the youngest student ever to attend Texas Christian University. Carson, who plans to become a quantum physicist, is taking calculus, physics, history, and religion in his first semester. Given that he was devouring chapter books by age two and attending high school by age five, the boy genius might reach his goal of attaining a doctorate degree before age twenty.

Anala Beevers

Anala Beevers of New Orleans learned the alphabet at four months of age and learned numbers in Spanish by the time she was eighteen months. Now, at four years old, she is one of Mensa's newest members.

Andrew Koonce

Andrew Koonce, fifteen, is a talented African American violinist from Atlanta. His list of awards and titles is impressive. As an eighth grader, he ranked first place at the Heritage Music Festival in Florida, winning the Maestro Award for best solo.

Zora Ball

At seven years old, Zora Ball has become the youngest person to create a mobile video game. The Philadelphia native developed the game using programming language Bootstrap, usually taught to students between the ages of twelve and sixteen to help them learn concepts of algebra through video game development.

Stephen R. Stafford II

While most of his peers slog through seventh grade, Stephen Stafford, thirteen, earns credits toward his premed, computer science, and mathematics degrees at Morehouse College.

Richard Turere

Living in Kenya's Masai Mara, Richard was given the task of finding a way to protect his family's cattle without harming any lions. Three weeks and much tinkering later, Richard had invented a system of lights that flash around the cow shed, mimicking a human walking around with a flashlight. His system is made from broken flashlight parts and an indicator box from a motorcycle.

Maya Penn

Maya Penn's small-business success story has been covered by *Forbes, Black Enterprise, Ebony, Huffington Post,* and Atlanta's *Fox 5 News.* She started out crafting ribbon headbands for family friends at age eight.

Though she works on the business just part time, Maya's ideas are on track to bring in about $55,000 in sales this year. She also vows to give away 10 percent of her profits to Atlanta-area charities. Penn, whose company is profitable, has donated $4,000 along with many volunteer hours. Now, at the age of fourteen, she is an eco-friendly fashion designer, coder, illustrator, writer, animator, and activist.

Daquan Chisholm

At twelve, enrolled in a program for talented youth, Chisholm was assigned to create something to make the world better. He designed a walkie-talkie, bulletproof helmet. "That was the first thing that came to mind, making the police feel safer walking the streets," said the Baltimore native.

Natalie Wambui

This ten-year-old Kenyan author has accomplished a lot in her first decade of life. She's an author, poet, and inspirational speaker all before reaching high school. After being frustrated by the negative things she read about Kenya, Wambui set out to write poems about people positively making a difference in her nation. So far she has authored three books: *Natalie's Poems, Kenya My Country, My Story,* and recently, *Extraordinary Kenyans Doing Extraordinary Things.* Natalie says her writings are meant to inspire others to overcome.

Message To Teachers

*We must make a paradigm shift in the way we teach
and learn. We are training more than educating.
The more differently we educate, the more different the
results will be. We are looking for different results!*

To Teachers

Now, your role will change. Teachers, you will want
to understand your new role in the learning
environment as a learner/facilitator/guide/leader/
consultant. The more teachers teach, the more teachers
learn—so, step back and allow learners to come forward.

You will enter this process where you and your learners
feel the most comfortable. Some of you are absolutely

ready for LTL. Others will engage at various levels. That's ok. But don't be scared. Your learners will help and raise your learning curve. Trust them and they will help you. These learners are accustomed to making life decisions that are far more complex than what to learn and how to learn it.

Review the Industrial and Knowledge Age chart on the following page.

Knowledge age characteristics of learning practices are contrasted with industrial age learning. When this is viewed as a continuum, we want to be more on the knowledge age side—learning through projects, problem solving, discoveries, and inventions for real-life/world use—to better students' lives and their communities to free them of racism and oppression. Learners are far more motivated when engaged in real-world learning and social justice actions.

Industrial age learning may still dominate too much in our schools. You want to move away from too much use of facts, drills, rules, and procedures. However, there will be times when some of those skills need to be developed.

When you free students to plan and teach, they will automatically move you to the knowledge age strategies.

Educational Technology/May-June 1999

Industrial and Knowledge age Characteristics of Teaching

Industrial Age	Knowledge Age
• Teacher as Director	• Teacher as Facilitator, Guide, Consultant
• Teacher as the Knowledge Source	• Teacher as Co-learner
• Curriculum-directed Learning	• Student-Directed Learning
• Time - Slotted, Rigidly Scheduling Learning	• Open, Flexible, On-demand Learning
• Primarily fact based	• Primarily Project and Problem based
• Theoretical, Abstract Principles & Surveys	• Real-world Concrete Actions & Reflections
• Drill & Practice	• Inquiry & Design
• Rules & Procedures	• Discovery & Invention
• Competitive	• Collaborative
• Classroom Focused	• Community Focused
• Prescribed results	• Open-ended Results
• Conform to Norm	• Creative Diversity
• Computers-as-Subject of Study	• Computers-as-Tool for all Learning
• Static Media Presentations	• Dynamic Multimedia Interaction
• Classroom - bounded Communication	• Worldwide - unbounded Communication
• Test-assessed by Norms	• Performance - assessed by Experts, Mentors, Peers & Self

Remember, the need for nurturing, caring, compassionate teachers cultivating the best in our children, while promoting justice and equality, always remains at the core of teaching and learning.

What Teachers Can Do—Use the Liberating Teaching and Learning Model

- ◆ Display expressions of sincere approval and warmth.
- ◆ Develop a relationship with your learners.
- ◆ Be fair, firm, and friendly consistently.
- ◆ Structure the classroom environment in such a way as to provide maximum opportunity for learners to manage themselves and to choose what and how to learn.

Apply LTL—You are one person and can't be expected to know it all and be everything to everybody. We need to move you from the front of the classroom, controlling everything, to the sides, and around the back of the classroom serving as a learner/facilitator/guide/consultant, liberating the brilliance and intelligence to shine in your learners as they take responsibility for their learning. **They will learn in ways that will allow them to survive, thrive, and contribute in our world like only they can.**

The more "how to do it" we give the learner, the more we get in the way. Let them SOAR!
—Bettye Haysbert

You are given a class of thirty to thirty-five elementary, middle, or high school students who bring many needs and concerns to the classroom. It is easy to become overwhelmed about what to do with the students and all of their needs. I know you have not been trained to successfully meet those needs (I think that is an impossible task).

I know because I am a teacher, and I have provided teacher professional development and taught you in colleges and universities. However, I do agree that it is very important to get to know your students (affect is very important); how to do it is the question. LTL is a simple, quick way to address the diverse needs of your learners.

The quickest way for you to learn about your students is for them to show you who they are, what they need to learn, and what they want to learn in order to be interested in the class and successful, surviving and thriving, contributing citizens in the world.

Eighty percent of you teachers in the United States are European American (EA), teaching a student population of 51 percent people of color. Seldom have you been taught the culture or history of your learners. Hence, the need for Liberating Teaching and Learning: because we can't wait another century or so for you to be given the education needed to meet diversity goals in the traditional ways—in college classes or professional development—only.

Get Help from Your Students

Get to know your students. Learn about:

- ◆ their backgrounds, where they are from, their life struggles, and delights;
- ◆ their family stories—as much as they want to share;
- ◆ their interests and hobbies;

- what they want to learn; and
- how they like to learn.

This can be done easily through their interactions with you, their interactions with teammates, and their selected projects.

Use their culture, experiences, interests, and background to personalize the teaching of concepts and skills. The curriculum and instruction support the middle and upper classes of our society, yet 51 percent of public school students are at or below poverty level. So, classroom instruction must fit the needs of learners who arrive at school each day.

Tell them about yourself. You may find the statements and questions in the Personal Cultural Reflections (below) helpful in describing your own culture. I've used this list many times in my classes. It will be helpful later when we talk about our culture. Tell what you want them to know. This can be shared over time.

- What are the ethnicities of yourself, your parents, and your grandparents?
- What is your culture (beliefs, values, worldview, behaviors)?

- What family influences have contributed most to shaping your culture?
- What are the rituals of your family (daily living, traditions, and practices)?
- What are your communication, behavioral, and learning styles?
- What aspect of your culture are you most or least proud of?
- How might your culture conflict with your learners' cultures?
- Where did you grow up?
- What are your hobbies and interests?
- If you are EA, acknowledge your privileged position in the world and your ethnic group as oppressors. The rest of us, because the school is oppressive, must be aware that we participate in the oppression of ourselves and others until we change it.

Banks and Banks (1993) say that teachers are human beings who bring their cultural perspectives, values, hopes, and dreams to the classroom. You also bring your prejudices, stereotypes, and misconceptions. Your values and views influence what and how you teach and the way that messages are communicated and understood by students. Take time to reflect on what you bring to the classroom. Elizabeth Martinez Smith's article "Racism: It Is Always There" shows us clearly where it is. Embark upon your journey of "unlearning racism."

Please know, my colleagues, AA learners are very much in tune with your feelings toward them. You can't hide them, so be reflective and true to yourself. Think about your biases, prejudices, stereotypes, and any racist tendencies you may or may not be aware of and work them out. If you don't like your learners, have low expectations of them, or don't want to be with them, they'll know—conflict is sure to rise, and little to no achievement will take place.

Because they don't care what you know, until they know that you care!
Tell them:

- about liberating teaching and learning;
- how you hold high expectations for them in learning;
- how teaching and learning will be turned upside down;
- how they will be given more responsibilities for what they learn and how to learn it (yeah, I know there are some things you must teach, but then learners are free to learn it their way—the key is to give choice in every assignment);
- how they will choose to learn what they want to learn—don't worry, you will cover what you need and more (maybe you don't even need to

cover what you think); we want them learning vs. covering material (you and your learners can work that out);

◆ how you and they will be coplanners and coteachers of lessons, taking ownership for their learning; and

◆ your classroom will be fair, just, safe, and nurturing for all learners.

You and they will benefit immensely by knowing each other's culture and history. So, liberate them to expand your knowledge through their choices and show you:

◆ who they are,

◆ what they like/dislike in curriculum and instruction,

◆ what they think and what's important to them,

◆ how they work best in the school environment, and most of all,

◆ how their brilliance and intelligence can shine.

When they are free to be themselves, they **SOAR!**

In the meantime, you are learning not only who your students are but new instructional strategies and curriculum choices that are appropriate for your class of learners.

I selected seven African Americans and one Latina, ranging in age from four to fifteen years, to share how they felt about coplanning and teaching with teachers, how they would change a lesson the teacher has taught, and how they would change their schools to make them better. The two youngest, the four-year-old and a six-year-old, were asked only three questions.

All the learners responded to the questions without any preparation and gave honest responses. Learners have answers and are ready to share them.

Four-year-old AA male:

1. Why is your favorite teacher your favorite?
   - She teaches me a lot and about numbers and how to share.
2. Name one thing that you like about your school.
   - Play time, especially bowling.
3. Name one thing you would change about school to make it better.
   - I would put a lamp in the middle of the classroom so that when it is dark outside my teacher and the kids could see better.

Note: His class has lots of light when the sun shines, but on an overcast day, it's darker, and the high recessed lights don't give enough light.

Six-year-old old Latina:

1. Why is your favorite teacher your favorite?
   - Because when we have our brain breaks, she gives us snacks.
2. Name one thing that you like about your school.
   - I like the mermaid stickers that I get from my Little Bob books.
3. Name one thing that you would change about school to make it better.
   - I would change recess—add one more.

The rest of the learners were asked the following questions.

1. Schools are changing like the rest of our world. Schools are moving from the teacher doing all the planning and teaching to you helping to plan and teach lessons. You would have a chance to tell what you wanted to learn and how you wanted to learn it.

Seven-year-old AA female:

1. What do you think about that?
   - I think that they are good.
2. Think about a lesson your teacher has taught. In one or two statements, tell how you would change that lesson if you were teaching it.

• I would change the way she does spelling. I would say the word and then pick someone to spell it.

3. Why is your favorite teacher your favorite?

• Because she is nice.

4. Name one thing that you like about your school.

• I like that we have share time.

5. Name one thing you would change about your school to make it better.

• I would change that we couldn't go to the bathroom during music class.

6. What is culture?

• I don't know.

Eleven-year-old AA female:

1. How do you feel about that change?

• I think it's a good idea, makes things easier, faster, and funnier.

2. Think about a lesson your teacher has taught. In one or two statements tell how you would change that lesson if you were teaching it.

• Cube fractions – I would explain the subject more. Write what you don't know on paper rather than on a whiteboard—can go back and check when needed.

3. What do you like about your favorite teacher?

• She gave help when I needed it and would answer questions with more examples when needed.

4. Name one thing that you like about your school.
   ◆ We have lots of activities, learning activities, and summer school if you want to attend.
5. Name one thing you would change about school to make it better.
   ◆ Maybe more field trips, more activities at lunch. Now we only have basketball and soccer. I would have more classrooms to come out at the same time. Now, we have 1–3, 4–6, and 7–8. I would change it to be K–3, 4–5, and then 6–8, the middle school.
6. What is culture?
   ◆ Different kinds of things that the family members do.

Eleven-year-old AA male:

(This learner later introduced a new way of doing decimals to his class that the teacher allows its use in the class.):

1. How do you feel about that change?
   ◆ Seems like a good idea. Children aren't just given things to do. They assign their own work, learn to find how they learn, learn to choose what they want to learn about the subject.
2. Think about a lesson your teacher has taught. In one or two statements, tell how you would change that lesson if you were teaching it.

◆ Historical realistic fiction lesson, watch a short film, write, and just read one book. I would change it to have the students read two books, determine what facts stay and what facts would go.

3. Why is your favorite teacher your favorite?

◆ Even though she was a little strict, she taught lessons in a way that you could understand. When questions were asked, she answered them the best she could.

4. Name one thing that you like about your school.

◆ Teachers doing a good job. They like for kids to enjoy and be interested in what they are learning.

5. Name one thing you would change about school to make it better.

◆ I would give students more independent work and also, when multiple students have the same questions, instead of answering the questions separately, answer to the whole class.

6. What is culture?

◆ How people are different where you're from, celebrations and beliefs that you have.

Fifteen-year-old AA female:

1. How do you feel about that change?

◆ I think it's a good idea to hear ways other than

how teachers teach. Students think outside of the box.

2. Think about a lesson your teacher has taught. In one or two statements, tell how you would change that lesson if you were teaching it.
   - Algebra: the Box method was used to solve an equation in class. It was easy, but I think there are other ways to solve it without the Box method. I would use the FOIL method, and there are other methods, I'm sure. I would use different methods.

3. Why is your favorite teacher your favorite?
   - The ways she taught things were very understandable.

4. Name one thing that you like about your school.
   - Funny kids.

5. Name one thing you would change about school to make it better.
   - I would like to see more activities: clubs, study clubs.

6. What is culture?
   - Culture is traditions, celebrations—how your people are.

Fifteen-year-year old AA female:

1. How do you feel about that change?
   - I like the change of children helping direct

what and how the class learns. But I also like it
when the teacher sets the course schedule.

2. Think about a lesson your teacher has taught. In
   one or two statements, tell how you would change
   that lesson if you were teaching it.
   - I cannot think of a lesson where I would have
     changed how the teacher taught the course.
3. Why is your favorite teacher your favorite?
   - She was fun and very entertaining. She has her
     students do a lot of project-based learning and
     working in small groups.
4. Name one thing that you like about your school.
   - I love my school because it is inclusive and
     welcoming to everyone.
5. Name one thing you would change about school
   to make it better.
   - Sometimes we have extended classes, and I would
     like to make them a little bit shorter. I would
     rather some classes be an hour rather than longer.
6. What is culture?
   - Culture is the history and use of things in their
     everyday lives; it can be related to food, art, or
     a lot of other things.

The responses from this small sample of learners speak
to how easy it is to change and how ready learners are to
contribute, when given the opportunity, to enhance their
learning environment. They are not empty vessels.

Liberating Teaching and Learning (LTL):

◆ expands your knowledge and instructional strategies exponentially;

◆ relieves you from the impossible—trying to satisfy each student's every need, alone; and

◆ frees your time for other matters that need your attention in the classroom.

You may be surprised how brilliant and intelligent your learners are, thereby changing your perceptions and expectations of them.

Boredom, and what are perceived as behavior problems, often diminish, because of student buy-in. They are meeting their learning needs. Their interests, motivation, time on task, and achievement increase tremendously.

You will benefit from reading what African American and other scholars of color are saying about students' cultural learning and behavioral styles, as you facilitate each learner to perform to his or her maximum potential.

I remember teaching you in colleges, universities, and professional development sessions how to include these valuable strategies and information in your teaching:

cooperative learning and multiple intelligences, differentiated instruction, and cultural learning styles, and African American history and culture.

Now we understand that when we liberate students to choose their best modes of learning, lessons are automatically differentiated (they will choose to support their strengths) and individualized; learners work in their cultural styles, and certainly their multiple intelligences are honored as they learn and teach each other their history.

When students have choice, they teach you who they are and what they are interested in through the choices they make. This is the best professional development you can receive, one-on-one, in real time, with an ongoing, built-in support system—your learners.

MESSAGE TO LEARNERS

A revolution is under way to change the way we structure teaching and learning in our classrooms, now!

You will lead the way in making this happen by using the revolutionary teaching and learning model mentioned earlier, Liberating Teaching and Learning (LTL).

Leading this way isn't new to us AAs.

♦ We led the way in the 1800s and 1900s when Carter Woodson, George Williams, W. E. B. Du Bois, and others started writing books to counter the negative images and lies that were being told about us.

- We led the whole civil rights movement for equal rights.
- We led the fight for integration in public schools.
- Then, in the '60s and '70s, we led the fight for equity and social justice in schools, colleges, and universities that required them to add Ethnic Studies to the curriculum and increase enrollment. Out of this was born the Black Student Unions (BSUs), organizations dedicated to unifying, uplifting, and empowering AAs on and off campuses.

We are making some progress in getting ethnic content into the curriculum, but school structure and instruction are basically the same.

LTL is advocating for deep structural change: turn it (the present structure) upside down. Don't worry—all learners are uplifted, especially people of color.

LTL allows your brilliance, intelligence, creativity, spontaneity, and resourcefulness, among other characteristics, to SOAR!
AA learners, you have been stifled for as long as you have been in school. It can be very hard to come to school each day:

- where nothing being taught (and no part of how it is being taught) reflects or honors who you are;

◆ where you seldom use your strengths or have opportunities to study your interests, history, and culture;

◆ where you are punished just because you require an interactive learning environment but are expected to sit and be attentive for long periods, while one person gives all the information and tells you how and what to think and how to behave. This controlling form of teaching has to stop. It works for no one. That is not how learning takes place. Learning requires interacting with curriculum and others.

Schools require this from you even though we know that "learning is the active construction of meaning, not a passive receptive process"—meaning, people learn best through interaction.

Seldom are you given knowledge and taught skills that you can use to make your life better—to help you to survive and thrive in life. In fact, most times the opposite happens. You are told that you don't contribute anything positive to this society now and never have, which is **not** true.

I encourage you to extend your reading beyond what is given to you in school. Learn about your culture and history. Use what is of interest to you among the recommended readings listed in this book, but read what interests you. Then **learn to read and view videos/movies critically at all times (especially textbooks) using the following questions as a guide.**

With new knowledge as the lens for examining racial and ethnic inequalities and stereotypes, read or view with these questions in mind to detect biases—loaded words/negative statements, misinformation, injustices, and inequalities. Add your own.

1. Whose truth is being privileged or "told"? Who is writing?
2. Who is missing?
3. What are the loaded words? (Negative words used to describe a person or group of people.)
4. How are people of color portrayed or treated? Positively or negatively?
5. Is information being accurately represented?
6. How would you respond to these biases?

Loaded words (below): words assigned value by people of European ancestry and used mostly by them in referring to people of color.

"Dark" Qualities	"White" Qualities
superstitious	scientific
abnormal	normal
emotional/angry	calm

colorful	bland
dark	air/blond
un-American	American
radical	conservative
illegal	legal/law abiding
dirty	clean
rude	polite
pagan	Christian
primitive/uncivilized/barbaric/savage	civilized
intellectually inferior	intelligent
subhuman	human

There are many, many others. That's called reading critically.

Too many of you are not taught to read by the magical cut-off point of third grade across the nation, so research tells us that you have a 70 percent chance of being in prison. Many Americans can't read. We could argue schools could do a better job for all their citizens. Many learners would profit from extending reading instruction through middle school. Or even into high school. Different reading skills are needed at various levels.

If you struggle with reading, go to www.readingourway.com and learn to read.

Know that you are different. Different is excellent. Learn about and embrace your differences. Educate

others about your differences. Thank God who made you. "Be you." He/she knows what she/he's doing. Don't personalize rejection. Don't allow your opinion of yourself to be colored by the opinion of those who fail to see your beauty, best qualities, and potential. Remember, it is their opinion—let them keep it.

However, you need to know your differences are perceived and treated as deficiencies, as scary, and entire industries are built based on your perceived differences, all to punish you for being different. We are aware no one is suspended, expelled, or punished more at school than you. Even preschoolers are suspended. This happens across the nation.

Preschoolers know the difference between themselves and European Americans—and not in a good way. They know the difference in the way they are treated, especially when they're being mistreated. Become aware of or review the work of Kenneth and Mamie Clark. Take a look at any of the Kenneth and Mamie Clark "Doll Test" experiments on YouTube. The experiment shows the effects of racism on children ages three to nine. The Clarks showed a Black and a White doll and asked which children preferred. The majority chose the White doll and assigned it positive characteristics, while assigning negative ones to the Black doll who looked like them.

Several doll tests have been done since then, and the results have been similar. Sadly, many of us are still expressing a level of self-hate. Let's just stop being manipulated. Remember the article before, "Racism: It Is Always There." You have been tricked/ brainwashed into believing negative things about you and those who look like you. Start your journey of unlearning self-hate. It won't take long. The truth will set you free.

Special Education

Special education has long been a dumping ground (punishment) for learners who learn and behave differently. Now, "behavior" schools have popped up and you represent the highest ethnic group in both.

I realized, when I first taught in special education, that you were not what was called "special needs." You were given a culturally biased test (still being used today) that you couldn't even read to determine that you needed to be placed in special education. You didn't have sufficient reading, writing, and math skills. I taught you to read, write, spell, think, listen, and do math. Some of you did better than some of the students in regular classrooms. When I tried to get the name changed from Educable Mentally Handicapped, the school district refused because they would lose their funding. I was astounded and vowed I would prove that it isn't the student that is a problem but, rather, the school system. You are going to help me prove this. You will take the opportunities given you to show what you know, to learn things that are of interest to you and empowering to you. Teach what you learn to others and SOAR!

Behavior Schools

I was shocked to see behavior schools. When I looked at the ethnicity of students, of course, I wasn't surprised that the majority were African Americans and Latinos.

The goal of one school, as stated in the student handbook, is to assist students in changing behaviors so they may successfully return to the regular campus. Students are placed in this school because of "misbehaving." What is misbehaving?

As I viewed the curriculum and instruction, I saw nothing that showed what would be done to determine why you are misbehaving the way you are and how you would be assisted in learning new behaviors. That leaves me to believe that you are simply removed from a large setting to a smaller one, given the same things with tighter control, yet expected to reach different results.

One rule in the school manual says, "Students will not sleep in class." My question would be "Why do they sleep in class?" Another was "Students will raise their hands to be recognized by the teacher before speaking." You are probably saying, "What's wrong with that?" When you learn about the cultural behavior styles of many AAs, you will notice that many of these learners are spontaneous and have high energy levels. They want to share quickly.

The classroom works against you when your natural behaviors are denied expression. You are expected to conform to another way of being. Read more about culture later in the book. It is the responsibility of the school to meet you where you are. It is not your responsibility to contort and deny yourself to meet structures that clearly work against you.

Special education and behavior school settings will especially benefit from LTL, and I would throw in some yoga classes for you, teachers, and everybody working at the behavior school.

But let's get back to "You are different." One obvious difference is the melanin in your skin. Melanin is much more than what gives you the beautiful blackness of your skin. Melanin helps your body to operate, be healthy, and much more. View the YouTube video "The

Real Magic of Melanin: Amazing Things You Don't Know," read Dr. Carol Barnes's *Melanin: The Chemical Key to Black Greatness,* and read "Be Thankful for Your Melanin" from Kushite Kingdom. Now, you won't understand all this right now, but as you continue to learn, you will. Keep reading and discussing. Your understanding and appreciation will grow.

This brings to mind one of my classes in Johannesburg, South Africa. The teachers were of mixed ethnicities and from various parts of Africa and Europe. Most were from Africa. Everybody was planning for the one weekend of shopping we all anticipated and participated in. Johannesburg is a really big modern city—shopping there is good.

So, teachers were wanting to find nice products that were not knockoffs. I didn't know what they really meant. I finally said, "What are you talking about, 'knockoffs'?" They all chimed in, "Anything that's an imitation, anything that's not real." They shopped over the weekend. When we returned on Monday, I asked, "Did you find what you were looking for, your non-knockoffs?" A resounding, "Oh yes," very excited.

We had discussed the fact that African people are the first people, yet we imitate others. I said to them, "You are the original people; then why do you imitate someone else? When you do that, you are imitating a knockoff. Instead of imitating a knockoff, spend that time accepting and appreciating your original self."

This is a simple example of what happens when people express their differences.

Perception and Perspective

- ◆ People are individuals, unique and different from each other.
- ◆ We come from different families, different ethnic backgrounds and cultures.
- ◆ We have had different personal experiences.
- ◆ We want to have different things from life and from each other.
- ◆ We have different dreams, wishes, and expectations.
- ◆ Therefore, we can respond differently to the same situation and still be right.

Look at the picture, then look at it with another person.

- ◆ What do you see in the picture?
- ◆ If you viewed this with others, why did some

people see a young woman while others saw an old woman? Is there a correct way to see the picture?

◆ Did you see anything else in the picture?
◆ What did you feel toward those who saw the picture the same way you did? Toward those who saw it differently?

Embrace your differences. Respect and value others, and learn from them.

Your time has come. Usually, the only time that you are free to show your strengths and skills in the school is in sports and occasional dramatic performances. Even though your skills and strengths are lauded outside, there is little-to-no attempt to transfer those skills and strengths into classroom achievement. I think it doesn't happen because of our narrow view of how learning occurs, and we want everybody to fit in the same box, the one European American men set up for themselves.

Schools expect you to become someone else when you enter the classroom. You are no longer free to be your brilliant, intelligent, creative, spontaneous, and resourceful self. Instead, you are controlled:

◆ told what to think;

- told how to behave—to sit in single-row desks for long periods of time and be quiet;
- told what to learn—which often is of little interest to you and has nothing to do with your greatness or what you need to survive and thrive as an oppressed people;

because someone has planned everything for you, not with your strengths, needs, or interests in mind, nor with any opportunity for your input.

Schools should fit the needs of the child. The child should not fit the needs of the school. Let's make the change.

LINK CLASSROOM AND OUTSIDE BRILLIANCE AND INTELLIGENCE THROUGH CULTURE

Bring your culture into the classroom

Courtesy: Bettye Chitman Haysbert, *Liberating Teaching and Learning*

We are going to revolutionize teaching and learning. You will work with your teacher and peers to bring that brilliance, intelligence, creativity, and resourcefulness into the classroom. Work together in cooperative/collaborative/communal groups. That's what research shows works for you. In fact, it works for most people, because "learning is the active construction of meaning, not a passive receptive process." In other words, "learning is interacting with the information to understand what it means for you vs. sitting quietly while someone else tells you what to think."

LTL combines with much-researched CL strategies as the instructional tools.

Don't wait for the teacher to learn how to do cooperative learning.

You learn, help her learn, and advocate for its use in the classroom.

There are many internet resources, including YouTube.

Culture Defined

What Is Culture? Both Explicit and Implicit

Here are two ways we look at culture: The tip of an iceberg—explicit or visible culture; the rest under the water and less seen—implicit, or hidden, culture.

The explicit/visible (there are other names) are the parts of culture that we see and participate in with the group who shares that culture, like their food, shelter, music, art, language, festivals, holidays, etc.

Then, implicit/hidden parts of culture are the parts of a group's culture we see least, understand least, and that can cause the most conflict when interacting with others. The implicit culture is what we're talking about in this book. It is the implicit cultural characteristics of students which are the least understood and likewise serve as barriers to learning and the foundations of much misunderstanding. This misunderstanding results in conflict between teachers and students.

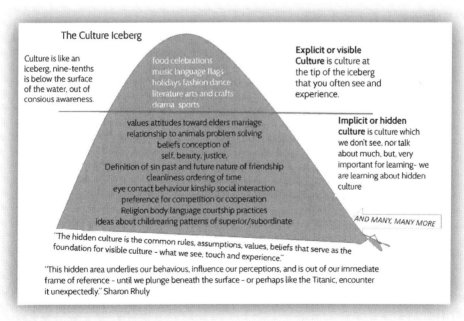

Courtesy: Bettye Chitman Haysbert, *Liberating Teaching and Learning*

Culture is the way a group of people live their lives.
They share behaviors, values, ideas, attitudes, traditions,
knowledge, beliefs, customs, rituals, practices, and language.
Culture governs all we do and how we act. It serves as a
guide in how to live and survive in our environment, how we
see ourselves in the world. All shaped by our experiences.

Nobles (1990) defines culture as "a general design for
living and patterns for interpreting reality." Culture is:

- a way of life that prepares us/students to learn,
  and function, in specific ways;
- learned, fluid, and changing;
- a unified system of information used for
  perceiving and understanding the world;
- patterns of learned behavior that are unique to a
  group of people.

People of the same ethnicity may not share the same
culture to the same degree.

People of different ethnicities can share the same
culture. Economics play a large part in determining
one's culture. People living at or below the poverty
line will have experiences that are similar, therefore,
regardless of their ethnicity; they are likely to share
similar cultural experiences. Their experiences and
culture will look least like the school's culture. School
culture represents the middle class and above.

Fifty percent of public school students are at or below the poverty level.

Cultural difference occurs when children have not had the experiences that provide them with the kind of information that is usable in school. They may have a storehouse of information, but it is not the background that is required for the curriculum.

Every culture is unique; no culture is "culturally deficient" or "culturally disadvantaged"; cultures are culturally different.

Stereotypes that develop because of "cultural illiteracy" and/or misinformation should be corrected through a study of cultures. Become:

- aware of the diversity of cultures in our society;
- knowledgeable about cultures;
- understanding of cultures (why people behave the way they do);
- accepting of people who are culturally different from oneself, not just tolerating them, but appreciating them.

Research shows that cultural patterns influence the way information is:

- ◆ perceived,
- ◆ processed, and
- ◆ utilized.

Culture Defines Who's Disabled

I want to share a story that comes from Thomas Armstrong's book *In Their Own Way*. Read about multiple intelligences in this book.

While our society favors linguistic (verbal, read, write) logical (thinking orderly) mathematical and intrapersonal (individualist) abilities, other cultures put a different emphasis on the seven varieties of intelligence.

In the Annang society of Nigeria, for example, musical and bodily-kinesthetic intelligences are highly developed. By the age of five, the children of that society can sing hundreds of songs, play numerous percussion instruments, and perform dozens of complex dances. Eskimo culture values spatial intelligence. They place a high survival value on noticing small differences in snow and ice surfaces. They don't want to be on the wrong side of a chunk of ice as it floats off into the sea. Eskimo children will score higher on tests of spatial intelligence than others of us.

In certain South Seas island cultures, the ability to build and steer a canoe and navigate it by the stars—requiring superior bodily-kinesthetic and spatial intelligence—is very important.

A highly literate person from our culture with superior linguistic or logical-mathematical intelligence might be at a real disadvantage in a South Sea island society. Without good spatial and bodily-kinesthetic skills, their "smarts" would be useless and they might even find themselves labeled "navigating disabled learners."

As you can see, different cultures require different ways of behaving that are important for what they need to survive.

Further, Armstrong tells the ancient story about a schoolteacher who hired an old man to take him across the river in a small boat. The teacher asked the old man whether the trip would be a difficult one. "I don't know nothing about it," replied the old man. The teacher, noticing the boatman's poor grammar asked him, "Haven't you ever been to school?" "No," said the old mariner. "Well then, half your life has been wasted," said the schoolteacher. The old man didn't say anything but started the journey. When they got about halfway across, a big storm came up and the boat began to rock to and fro. The crusty sailor turned to the teacher and asked him if he knew how to swim. The teacher said he didn't, to which the old man replied, "In that case, your whole life is wasted, for we are sinking!"

Ability in one situation can be a disability in another. Very important!

Different cultures foster and value different ways of learning and behaving that are consistent with what they need to survive.

Our school culture is determining that AA and Latino students and anyone else who learns and behaves differently are disabled and need a "special setting." Nothing is **wrong** with you; rather, the school system is **not** designed for your success.

CULTURAL
CHARACTERISTICS OF
MANY AFRICAN AMERICANS

Here, some comparisons are made between African American and European American culture because of the widespread belief that African Americans and European Americans should operate the same. No. We are different. Because EAs' culture dominates, some expect that you should behave the same as they—*not so!* Why would the oppressed and the oppressor operate the same? Only when you want to oppress yourself.

Note: Understand, any comparisons to EA learners are made here to support the uniqueness of AA learners' behavior and learning needs, not valuing one over the other.

Since the majority of teachers in our schools are EAs (80 percent), it becomes critical to show the differences between the two cultures to gain a better understanding of your needs and for EA teachers to understand their culture. When we do this, we eliminate the expectation that you will behave in the same manner as White students. When you do not, you will avoid being punished just for **being you.**

These are cultural characteristics that **African Americans generally share** and **Whites do not.** Remember, schools were set up for the benefit of EAs. AA cultural characteristics would not be a part of how the EA schools operate.

Boykin (1978), Hilliard (1985), and many other scholars characterize the African American culture as:

- highly affective—shows feelings and emotions;
- showing a sense of vitality—life, strength, activity, energy;
- resilient—showing toughness, ability to bounce back and to protect self from difficult experiences;
- full of verve/depth of feeling—high levels of stimulation, highly charged and loud expressions (you always hear, you are too loud and also impulsive);

- ◆ physically interactive—involves participating with others;
- ◆ orally communicative—expresses ideas with spoken language, but also uses the body to communicate;
- ◆ active-learning focused—(very important) learns best by being actively involved, especially in groups;
- ◆ cooperatively interdependent—peer oriented, dependence on each other in learning and play;
- ◆ spiritual—concerned with the soul and spirit, seeks happiness;
- ◆ rhythm focused and full of movement.

Your culture is full of life, with lots of interaction and energy. Therefore, your achievement increases when you are allowed to express your culture, especially when learning in teams/groups.

Let me share a story about being too loud. After one of my teaching assignments in Johannesburg, South Africa (SA), I made a trip to Durban, SA. Durban is a beautiful city on the Indian Ocean. It is the third largest city in South Africa after Johannesburg and Cape Town. I was invited to the home of one of the hotel workers. We had to take two long bus rides to her township. The trip was great. I met her mother and daughter and some of the people in the township. After a delicious meal prepared by her mother, we headed back to the hotel. On our way back to the hotel, I asked my new friend why wouldn't she move to the city now that it was legal to live wherever they wanted (apartheid has been abolished—read if not familiar with this). She replied, "I like living where I live because we are loud, and we're not going to change our traditions to live next to White people." Hmm, how refreshing and insightful.

Teachers, I hope you are beginning to better understand who the AA learners are and what they need to be successful in the classroom, that when you see some of these cultural characteristics, you are not "baffled" or "intimidated" by the learners' behavior. This understanding can eliminate the negative judging of African American children and questioning of their academic abilities and attitudes toward learning.

Remember, teachers, LTL will allow you to continue to learn from the learners as you work together to ensure these learners' brilliance and intelligence are showing—and they are soaring. You may want to explore your own culture. I am reminded of one of my EA students who was a teacher in the San Francisco Unified School District, commenting after completing my class on Cultural Learning Styles, at San Francisco State University, "I will never see AA students as White students in Black skin again."

It becomes clear that the learning difficulties of African American students, as well as others, have their base more in cultural incompatibilities than incapabilities.

Let's take another look.

Black Children and Their Learning Styles

Schools support analytical learners and push out relational learners. Examine the school below.

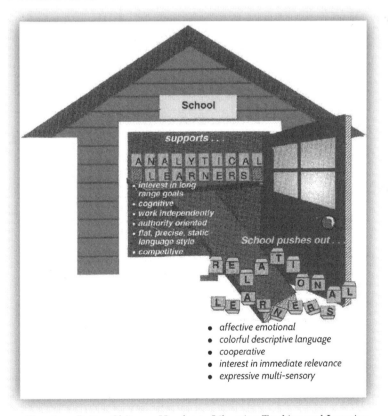

Courtesy: Bettye Chitman Haysbert, *Liberating Teaching and Learning*

It is the school that will change—not the learner. The learner has what is needed to succeed. Schools need to pull out of them what is inside and schools must adapt to the students who show up, not the other way around. Learning must start where a learner is and then grow and expand. United States public schools value the analytical learning styles, which value spoken and written language as used by the middle and upper classes and emphasize curriculum important to the lifestyles of EAs.

AA learners, on the other hand, usually are proficient in the relational learning styles, which emphasize visual and audio stimuli, the affect/emotions, feelings, interaction, and oral language.

Learning is best experiential. Janice Benson's book *Black Children: Their Roots, Culture, and Learning Styles* helped me to understand our culture.

Lots of research supports the notion that AAs have a distinct culture rooted in African culture and that it is different from EA culture. Our schools have been designed to support EA culture.

Adair (1984) says that the White-oriented educational system has been developed and tailored around the history, culture, and lifestyles of White America.

Woodson (1933) says that the so-called modern education, with all its defects, does others so much more good than it does the Negro, because it has been worked out in conformity to the needs of those who have enslaved and oppressed the weak people.

Woodson told us as far back as 1933 that our American public schools were not designed to educate us but to train us. So it's time for **radical change**. Yet another reason for LTL.

If instruction is to be effective, it must match the cognitive and behavior styles of all children to increase their chances for school achievement. Public school curricula must also include the cultural behaviors, values, and cognitive styles children bring to school.

Curriculum must reflect the experiences and history of people of color. We must liberate learners and teachers to learn and teach differently in order to ensure the change we seek happens—and quickly.

Our schools leave out the concerns and interest of large numbers of students when creating school-improvement plans or increasing achievement, and we don't connect it to school failure. Learners are more motivated and excited about learning when the environment reflects them.

In his eight-year study of schools, John Goodlad (1983) found that "schools are trying to improve themselves when they have not determined how balanced the curriculum [is] for each student, [or] the relevance of school to students' lives." This is still not being done in too many places. Here is one more reason why LTL is needed.

The more knowledge you have about the learner, the better. However, it is unlikely that you are going to be able to match your instruction to all learners' needs and ensure existing curricula are meaningfully inclusive of all ethnic groups, by yourself. Coplan and teach with your learners. Let's continue.

Hilliard (1985) says the cultural characteristics generally shared by Black children that Whites do not share include:

◆ high levels of energy, impulsive interrupting, and loud talking.

Teachers who are not aware that these characteristics are natural, and not disruptive to Black children, sometimes allow this behavior to negatively influence their judgment of a Black student's academic ability.

Boykin (1992) reports research that Black children are more:

- socially active, peer oriented, and physically active, suggesting the need for a classroom environment that offers frequent opportunities for changes in task.

I suppose you are able to see the stark differences between some AAs' and EAs' culture in areas that make a difference in how we need to structure teaching and learning. Remember, schools are set up to support EAs' culture, and because of that mere fact, schools work *against* AAs' culture.

A Comparison of African American and European American Culture

- **African Americans'** behavior tends often to be high key, animated, interpersonal, confrontational, intense, dynamic, and demonstrative.
- **European Americans** tend often to be low key, dispassionate, impersonal, nonchallenging, and emotionally restrained.
- When **Black** students present their ideas in this high-energy style, teachers consider them to be aggressive and lacking in self-control. As a result, they are often disciplined.
- **African Americans** often show differences between an argument used to debate difference of opinion and an argument used to vent anger and hostility.

- When **European Americans** debate difference of opinion, they often use discussion that lacks affect (feeling/emotion) and confrontation.
- Many **African American** students are punished for "fighting" when they are simply arguing to vent their anger. For **Whites**, fighting is a verbal as well as a physical confrontation.
- **African Americans** consider fighting physical action only.
- **African Americans** more readily question the authority of knowledge or ideas that have been published or certified by experts (people who don't look like them).
- When **African American** students interject their personal viewpoints and question the findings of published authors, teachers infer that African Americans are illogical, unintelligent, and naïve.
- **African Americans**, in a heated discussion, frequently make their points whenever they can enter the discussion. Deference is given to the person who considers his or her point more urgent.
- Turn taking is the style of **European Americans**, who usually raise their hands to be recognized. (Remember the earlier picture of the old classroom and children raising their hands.)
- Teachers find **Black** learners impolite, aggressive, and boisterous when they cut off another student

or fail to restrain themselves so that every student can have a turn to talk.

- **African Americans** hesitate to share information about their personal lives.
- **European Americans** often begin their conversations with queries concerning one's occupation, place of residence, number of children, and birthplace.
- **African American** students may not maintain constant eye contact with teachers as do **White** students.
- Often **African American** children are accused of not paying attention when they are.
- **African American** students are more likely than **European American** students to challenge or test school personnel because of beliefs that leadership is derived not from position, credentials, or experience but through personal attributes of strength, forcefulness, persuasiveness, and generosity.

Kochman (1981)

"Regardless of who exhibits which cultural characteristics, current data support the belief that not only do African Americans have a culture that is distinct, African-based, identifiable, and more ancient than European culture, but the two cultures are incongruous and contradictory. Boykin (1992) (Incongruous means not the same/out of harmony/opposite of each other.)".

This is critical information. EA culture being opposite from AAs' culture speaks to some—I would say, much—of the reason for AA learners' disproportionate suspension and expulsion rates, special education placements, and now behavior school placements for "misbehaving." Now that you both, teacher and learner, have a better understanding of what we're working with, I know you will begin to use LTL immediately.

Again, it becomes clear that the learning difficulties of African American students as well as other students of color have their base more in cultural incompatibilities than incapabilities!

Boykin (1986) described the "triple quandary" of Black Americans by stating that they operate simultaneously in three realms:

- the African-based Black culture,
- the mainstream Eurocentric culture, and
- the oppressed minority.

CULTURE OF THE HOME, SCHOOL, AND PLACE OF WORSHIP

R ecently, the school failure of learners of color has been explained in terms of a mismatch between the culture of the home and that of schools. We know that our schools reflect the culture of EAs. So, of course there is a mismatch. We can see how likely this is with AA learners and others.

Let's take a look at the home, school, and place of worship and the impact these important institutions have on our lives. They help to shape who we are and are the most socializing institutions in our lives. I know that many of you may not attend a place of worship, and that's ok.

Home Culture

The home is the first place where you can be who you are culturally. This is where your culture is developed and nurtured. The place where you first begin to learn and be socialized (how you are taught to behave).

Your home will have some of these characteristics. Many homes maybe:

- **people focused**;
- caring, protected environments where people express their feelings and emotions;
- environments where there is a great deal of human interaction;
- small spaces shared by large and extended families;
- environments where family members are passed from lap to lap as babies, fostering people connection;
- social environments where members may play with people as opposed to toys only;
- places of verbal interplay—rapping, joking, and teasing;
- **places with lots of stimulation;**
- places where you are active and expend lots of energy in a variety of activities;

- places where you enjoy an abundance of intensity and variation with music, song, and dance;
- places where high a noise level exists;
- places where you may spend lots of time watching TV;
- places where there may be a heavy dependence on dance and music in everyday activities;
- places where you may enjoy spontaneity—create when and how you wish—I'm reminded of the YouTube sensation, brilliant seventeen-year-old Daryon Simmons, who was just sitting in his house and decided to "do something." In a few minutes, he created (wrote lyrics for and choreographed) the dance "DLOW Shuffle" that went viral. I saw him appearing on TV teaching the "Shuffle" to the world. This kind of brilliant, spontaneous inventiveness is present in many, many AA learners all over the country.

We teachers don't know how to transfer that brilliance into school curriculum and learning. That's ok. Free learners to show you by letting them decide how to learn what you need to teach. Allow them to put their spin on curriculum and instruction. As one of my eleven-year-old interviewees said, "It will be funnier."

The takeaway here is that when you have grown up in a people-focused, highly stimulated environment, you have become accustomed to learning and behaving in that kind of environment. So, if schools plan to support this learner, an interactive, people-focused setting would be most appropriate. LTL would fit the bill because LTL acknowledges that no two classrooms are the same, just as no two homes are the same. Learners will be able to **match and bridge** the home and school cultures.

Place of Worship Culture

Your culture is supported in the church. We choose the churches that best represent our culture. Not all African American churches operate the same, but most will operate similar to this.

- The church is people focused and has lots of stimulation.
- It is a caring and nurturing environment.
- The minister teaches and preaches with gusto, vitality, and emotion.
- Members engage with the minister in what is referred to as "call and response"—a form of talk back to the minister, signaling an agreement. This kind of spontaneity is expected, along with reading-singing, clapping, stomping, shouting, and praise dancing. There is no judgment for the way you want to worship.

- You can get up at will and go to the bathroom or change seats.
- Music completes the day—usually many different instruments and at least piano, organ, drums (rhythm and movement), and great vocalists.
- You have opportunities to make presentations— dramatic plays, recitations, and spoken word.

Your home culture will usually mirror your place of worship culture.

School Culture

Now, this is a different story. Your culture is not supported in the school. Although many schools do allow time to interact and release energy, we have a long way to go. This is another reason why **liberating teaching and learning** is so important. Actually, LTL works best for most people because learning is interactive.

Again, the school:

- is object focused—tasks, tools, pencil, paper, books, educational hardware, stations, centers, and technology;
- is focused on teacher activities—how and what to learn and how to behave;

- promotes isolation—little human interaction—
  and forbids speech without permission;
- supports conformity—crushes freedom, creativity,
  enthusiasm, and spontaneity;
- supports rigidity—few avenues for energy release
  without permission;
- requires long periods of sitting—one assignment,
  one way—with no diversity;
- is a sterile environment and too quiet;
- requires you to sit quietly and look only at the
  teacher;
- thinks the teacher is the only one with
  knowledge—neither your knowledge,
  experiences, nor strengths are used;
- has nothing or little that looks like or acts like
  your culture; and
- watches and judges you unfairly on many
  occasions.

Yet again, it becomes clear that your learning difficulties
have their base more in cultural incompatibilities
(mismatches) than incapabilities (lack of ability)!

All knowledge or curriculum textbooks and tests are
based on EA culture, perspectives (the way they see
things), and experiences. We must bring learning
experiences both in terms of curriculum and in terms
of instruction to reflect the experiences of AAs and

other students. Such knowledge is important if schools are to help you to maximize your human potential and your individual abilities.

Critical Incident for Cultural Understanding-Help Solve This Challenge

A seven-year-old AA male, Kamal, has been referred to a study team to determine whether he should be referred to special education placement. His mother has two other children, who are doing better than Kamal. She has been to the school several times for Kamal's "misbehaving." His teacher thinks he constantly misbehaves, shouts out answers before he's called on, talks loudly, can't sit still, is always tapping or humming, and has low achievement. You are asked to sit in on his Individualized Education Plan (IEP). You accept. Now, based on your knowledge about the role culture plays in school, tell how you would advise the mother and IEP team. What factors would you look at and why?

AFFECTIVE DOMAIN VERSUS COGNITIVE

These areas of learning are used to guide how we plan and write our lesson plans. We usually start with the cognitive (thinking about the task first), move to the affective (how to engage learners emotionally and how learners will feel about this lesson), and finally, consider what physical interaction or involvement is needed.

So, I say, instead, emphasize the domains of learning in this order: affective, psychomotor (physical), and cognitive. Why? AA learners (and a lot of people) are highly affective and need interaction in the learning experience. Most learners will benefit from the order listed below:

- Affective learning
- Psychomotor (physical), or behavioral learning
- Cognitive learning through reading textbooks and doing written assignments

To motivate student learning, the affective domain—emotion, attitude, and motivation—must be engaged.

The **affective learning domain** involves our emotions toward learning. If you are not interested, if your needs are not being met, no learning takes place. Bloom and Furst say it includes the manner in which we deal with things emotionally, such as feelings, values, appreciation, enthusiasms, motivations, and attitudes.

The **psychomotor (physical) learning domain** involves how to include activity in the lesson.

The **cognitive learning domain** involves intellect—the understanding of information.

In Benjamin Bloom's "Human Characteristics and School Learning," schools are **biased in favor** of the **cognitive learner,** who:

- learns easily the way most teachers teach,
- is supported in their way of learning and

behaving, through instructions, and reading textbooks and doing written assignments.

These are the students who are supported to be academic achievers, who are likely to complete college, become teachers, and perpetuate the cycle. This style is associated mostly with EAs.

Schools are **biased against affective and psychomotor (physical) learners**. The affective learner:

◆ learns best through group interaction,
◆ is people oriented,
◆ gathers information informally, and
◆ does not function optimally in a quiet (so-called) orderly environment.

The psychomotor (physical) learner needs:

◆ to have activity and movement for optimum learning conditions, and
◆ to have things to touch, feel, and manipulate.

This learner does not conform to mandates to sit still and concentrate (Decker 1983).

It is important to note that teacher warmth, respect, and enthusiasm (affect) are important actions and have been found to be highly related to student achievement. Learners improved their conduct and school attendance when taught by a teacher who liked and put learners first (rather than a teacher who put assignments and things first), a teacher who was kind, optimistic, understanding, adaptable, and warm.

When this knowledge is applied in the classroom, learner needs are met, and less so-called behavior problems arise. **All of this means, it's ok to express our humanity, and inject some love, in education.**

One of my favorite sayings about learners is "They [learners] don't care what you know until they know that you care."

Feelings are always there in any learning situation and should be acknowledged. You show up to the learning environment as a whole individual; you bring all of yourself. You like to be seen as your whole self, and when you see that your thoughts, feelings, experiences, and culture are viewed as important in school, then school becomes important to you. We can't continue to think that you should like to come to a place every day that offers you nothing good about yourself. In fact, much too often, you are told and shown that you are worth little:

◆ You don't know how to behave.

- ◆ You never contributed anything positive to the advancement of the world.
- ◆ You can't learn.

The list goes on. The message is that something is wrong with you. (Although this is NOT true!) Seldom are you validated, lifted up.

Don't lose sight of the fact that we are oppressed people in this country, in these schools, and are attempting to be educated by the oppressor: 80 percent of teachers in this country are EAs, and even teachers of other ethnicities are oppressors, without knowing it, when they participate in the educational system the way it is presently designed.

Humanistic education, according to Freire, is a process of liberation from the oppressive system where teaching is done to the learners—rather than helping them be active participants in the teaching and learning process.

I feel that education should start with assessing the basic needs of humans, and that should be the foundation upon which instructional programs are built. When our learners are free to choose what and how they want to learn, they will automatically create a task that will begin with the affect, physical, and cognitive domains of learning, because those are their needs.

Learners, you don't have to wait for teachers to be able to plan lessons to meet all your needs and interests. Impossible task anyway. Plan and teach each other. Don't allow others to tell you that you can't do this. Yes, you can! Many have very low expectations of you.

A study states that 50 percent of publicly educated children live at or below the poverty level. Schools' instructional practices and curriculum are aimed at middle-class learners and above. We give the middle-class and above students an advantage in the classroom and never close the gap with the low socioeconomic students. This situation is made worse by the fact that most teachers (80 percent), in the United States, are EA and don't likely know these learners. Some don't even like the learners. LTL addresses all these issues—makes it easy. Teachers, free your learners to be teachers as you become more of a learner/facilitator/guide/consultant. "The more the teacher teaches, the more the teacher learns."

INSTRUCTIONAL STRATEGIES AND CURRICULUM

The second part of LTL is cooperative learning (CL)—I call CL Academic Teams (ATs). No other instructional strategy has been researched as much as CL, and it consistently proves to be effective for ALL children, especially African Americans and Latinos.

What It Is

CL is a cooperative interactive learning environment where students work together, contributing equally, in small heterogeneous groups, on academic tasks. Within such groups, students are encouraged to:

- share ideas,
- help each other learn,
- pool resources,
- share discoveries,
- justify their thinking,
- and critique each other's ideas.

CL/ATs satisfy the learning needs of those who need to interact—talking, moving about, making decisions about assignments, supporting each other (the affective part)—while completing an academic task. They bridge the affective and physical to the cognitive.

Research on CL suggests, overwhelmingly, that when students work together in small groups the following happen:

- Learning improves—and to an equal extent in both elementary and secondary schools; in urban, suburban, and rural schools; and in diverse subject matter areas.
- Problem-solving skills are enhanced.
- Social and racial relationships improve, and students learn to like and respect each other.
- Self-esteem improves.
- Students have a more positive attitude toward school.

You will have fun with the many different ways to use CL/ATs.

One of the most important findings to come from the cooperative learning research is the strong achievement gains among learners of color in cooperative classrooms.

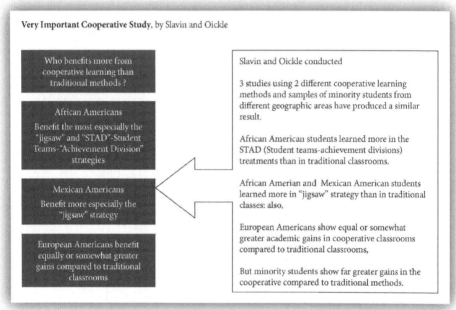

Very Important Cooperative Study, by Slavin and Oickle

Who benefits more from cooperative learning than traditional methods ?

African Americans
Benefit the most especially the "jigsaw" and "STAD"-Student Teams-"Achievement Division" strategies

Mexican Americans
Benefit more especially the "jigsaw" strategy

European Americans benefit equally or somewhat greater gains compared to traditional classrooms

Slavin and Oickle conducted

3 studies using 2 different cooperative learning methods and samples of minority students from different geographic areas have produced a similar result.

African American students learned more in the STAD (Student teams-achievement divisions) treatments than in traditional classrooms.

African Amerian and Mexican American students learned more in "jigsaw" strategy than in traditional classes: also,

European Americans show equal or somewhat greater academic gains in cooperative classrooms compared to traditional classrooms,

But minority students show far greater gains in the cooperative compared to traditional methods.

Courtesy: Bettye Chitman Haysbert, *Liberating Teaching and Learning*

More important benefits of working in cooperative/ collaborative/academic teams:

◆ Cultural needs are met.
◆ Students are more motivated.
◆ Understanding is enhanced.
◆ Greater retention results.
◆ Critical thinking skills are developed from real-life problem-solving situations.

- Listening and speaking skills are sharpened.
- Social skills are learned.
- Students get to know and support classmates.
- Students have an increased interest in school.
- Acceptance and understanding increase among children who are labeled with disabilities and their less-impaired classmates.
- When learning in cooperative learning/academic teams, students like school more than their peers who are not allowed to work together, are better able to interact appropriately with others, and are able to understand another person's point of view.

Additionally, students who are struggling with anger or social or family issues would have a safe place to discuss these struggles and develop ways to address them, teaching them how to solve real-life problems. Students make themselves available for each other, especially since being lonely and being bullied are high on many students' concern lists.

Teachers and learners, as you can see, you are able to use LTL and cooperative learning to meet your teaching and being learning needs.

Cooperative learning works. As one who has provided cooperative-learning professional development in school districts across the nation, and has used it in all my college and university classes, nationally and internationally, I have seen the positive effect on all learners, especially African Americans and Latinos.

How to Use Liberating Teaching and Learning (LTL)

LTL is very simple; don't overthink it. Relax. Step back and free learners to step forward. I know some of you feel constrained by mandated curriculum coverage, feeling that if student concerns are not in the text, you'll get off schedule. Seriously evaluate what you must teach and let learners have choice in what and how they learn. But know that they will learn so much more than what is required for curriculum coverage.

Regular experience in selecting, designing, implementing, and managing their own learning will enable them to become independent and prepare them for a lifetime of self-education and empowerment.

LTL is a simple two-part teaching and learning strategy.

1. Liberating: It frees the teacher and learner to coplan and coteach any lesson, at any time, in any subject, so learners can use their culture, history, strengths, and interests as part of the curriculum.
2. It uses CL/ATs to provide instruction. Learners

interact and teach each other. It acknowledges the students' prior experiences and uses them to bridge the distance between the school curriculum/methods and the cultural background of the students.

Examples of Lessons for Liberating Teaching and Learning

I guard against giving too much "how to do it," because it puts me back into the position of being the only one with the knowledge. No, you and your learners know how to do this.

When Teaching Prescriptively

The Teacher Learner Workshop
Here are some suggestions for how to teach when you want leaners to learn skills, when the lesson is prescriptive, *meaning:*

- This is something they need to know.
- This is something you need to teach.
- You can free them to tell how they want to learn it. You don't know what works best for each learner. You empower them, and that is motivating.

Your goal is for them to learn: the easiest way to reach that goal is to liberate students to decide how they will learn the task.

Example: CL/ATs (if you decide to be trained, take the training with your learners—more on this later).

- Form CL/Academic Teams of four. (You and your learners might need training in cooperative learning.)
- The goal of the lesson is to teach the short sound of the letter "a." (A lesson in phonics requires that **you, teacher,** teach the letter sounds.) In this lesson, it's the short sound of the letter "a."
- Introduce the sound of the letter, to ensure learners know how to make the sound correctly.
- But free them to decide how they will learn that sound.

They may want to:

- find and use their own word to cue them (you use "at," and they use "as" or "am," etc.);
- find a picture that gives them a clue, if necessary; etc.

When teaching rules/equations—this is prescriptive also, meaning this is something **you/teacher** need to teach or learners need to know—then free them to decide how to learn it. Again, free learners to decide **how** they want to learn. You don't know what works best for all of them. When learning comes from them, it's retained and is learned faster. You'll have a lot of different learning choices being used by learners, which ensures that students will learn from each other.

They may want to:

- put the rule/equation into their own words (check to ensure that the meaning remains the same),
- create a rhythm for it,
- illustrate it,
- write it several times,
- create a poem, or
- simply repeat it many times.

The list is endless. They will choose what works for them (to ensure that their interests and cultural needs are met), and learning will happen faster with no retention problems.

Allow time in the learning experience for teams of learners to teach each other what they have learned and how they designed their learning. This is very important because peers are very influential and can learn a lot from each other.

Liberate them so their brilliance, intelligence, creativity, and resourcefulness can shine, and they can SOAR!

When Teaching Concepts

Here are some tips on how to teach when you want learners to learn concepts or everything else:

> *Remember, coplan and coteach. It is in this process when you both decide what each will do to teach and learn the lessons. Find ways to give learners choice in every lesson. This is so liberating for both of you, and learning expands exponentially. Motivation is high, and time on task increases—much of the "misbehaving" is eliminated.*

Example:
Goal: The Civil Rights Movement (or anything else)

- ◆ Form CL/academic teams (ATs)
- ◆ This is the time when learners will have many opportunities to study what is of interest to them. Liberate them!
- ◆ Don't worry. They will learn far more than you planned for them to, because instead of everybody learning only about the same aspect of the movement, learners gain a more holistic view of the period from the diverse interests of teams.

- Learners can pursue their own history—i.e., usually the Latinos, Asian Americans, and Native Americans are left out of this discussion.
- Each CL/AT decides what area of the Movement they want to study.

Help teams clarify what they want to learn from their study. It will be fantastic.

- Learners may study aspects of this subject that the teacher may be reluctant to discuss or may never have thought of.
- Allow time at the end of the study for learners to teach other classmates what they have learned.
- Learners work in their preferred cultural styles.
- They present multicultural perspectives, and certainly their multiple intelligences are honored.
- When students have choice, they bring out the diversity in the class and contribute to a rich, dynamic learning environment like never before.

I used LTL with college and university students who were teachers. My traditionally three-unit, semester-long courses were taught in a condensed amount of time. Teachers would be taught over a two- to three-week time period. In those classes, the curriculum was more prescriptive (less flexible) than the instruction. CL was always used because of the support learners needed and how quickly they needed to really learn the content.

However, within the groups, learners had complete control over how they managed their assignments—using their interests and strengths. Since there were concepts I needed to teach, learners had the freedom to learn them the way they wanted while being supported by their CL/AT members.

For their final project (which served as an assessment), learners had to "Show What You Know"—they were **free** to demonstrate what they had learned. This way, I could evaluate what they really knew, because they took what had been given to them, constructed their own meaning, and gave it back in a way that was usable for them. That learning will not be forgotten.

I'm reminded of teaching in South Africa, when, after a visit to the museum, learners were told to decide how they would present their responses. (They didn't get any more directives than that.) This is one of the many times when the less "how to do it," the better, unless you are teaching skills.

Their experiences were told through poems, illustrations/drawings, PowerPoint presentations, and storytelling. They set themselves up as a "gallery walk," and other learners who had also visited that museum walked to each station and were taught by their peer, while having their learning reinforced. Learners planned and taught this in one day. You really get to see what they learned, what was of interest to them, and how they like to present that knowledge.

For a final project in a course in Kuwait, one previously quiet teacher did something we least expected. She sang a song using what she had learned to the tune of the Australian National Anthem. We gave her a standing ovation. I could have missed that opportunity if I had told the class what to do: i.e., write a paper, etc. Powerful learning comes from these learning experiences.

When given these kinds of final projects and freedom to diversify in the classroom, you and your learners enjoy the most enriching learning environments.

Key: when you must teach the what (curriculum), free them to do the how (instruction). Always give choice.

Brandt (1986) suggests the inclusion of issues of racism in the curriculum and elimination of didactic and individual instruction. Instead, include collaborative classrooms where the teacher is consultant, facilitator, and provoker. The teacher critically analyzes racist curricula in an effort to design an antiracist one that challenges racism, sexism, and classism. The goals of antiracist teaching are justice and the liberation of the oppressed and the oppressor. The oppressor is a critical inclusion. Memi (1967) asserts that oppression justifies itself through oppression: the colonizer can only exonerate himself in a systematic pursuit of the dehumanization of the colonized (oppressed).

PROFESSIONAL DEVELOPMENT (PD)- TURN IT UPSIDE DOWN

The Teacher Learner Workshop

Turn it upside down: teachers, when you are to receive PD that deals with concepts and skills you are expected to learn and teach to your learners, then **select some learners to go with you** or have PD presented to your entire class (applies to kindergartners through twelfth graders).

Key: If you are going to use the knowledge and skills with your learners, select some learners to go with you. The more eyes and ears, the better. They will help you take in the information, make it suitable for themselves, and teach it to their peers, and you will have built-in coaches all year.

Because present teacher training presupposes an understanding of children of different cultures (not true, as is shown through this conversation), the training must be geared to the unique culture of the children in their classes, school, and society.

In my study of effective teachers, teachers said, "Traditionally 'experts' have been brought in to give PD to you, but trainers are not always in touch with what you and your students' needs are at the school. Trainers traditionally have not met individual needs through the same level of training being given to everyone. After leaving the training session, failed attempts may be made to transfer the knowledge to the classroom, and often, not enough coaching is provided to you until the skills are sufficiently developed."

Teachers, I have provided professional development for you many, many times and taught you at colleges and universities around the world. Yes, I and others have expected you to be able to come to a class or professional development sessions, receive information, and use it immediately in your classrooms. Some of you are able to do that, and many others are not.

I remember when we expected you to plan a lesson to include all these strategies:

- cooperative learning,
- multiple intelligences,
- differentiated instruction,
- cultural learning styles, and
- the history and culture of all learners.

That's a lot. However, when teaching and learning are liberated:

- lessons are automatically differentiated and individualized;
- learners work in their preferred cultural styles;
- learners present multicultural perspectives, and certainly their multiple intelligences are honored; and
- automatically, learners use their history and experiences as the base for learning.

When students have choice, they bring out the diversity in the class and contribute to a rich dynamic learning environment. You learn so much about your learners and gain new knowledge as well.

When teachers were asked, in a survey, about the things they were most concerned about regarding PD, the major topics were:

- how to transfer and implement instructional insights gained in the professional development setting to a classroom of diverse learners,

- how to get help in the classroom to know whether they are implementing correctly,
- how to address not having enough long-range in-class support—coaching,
- how to gain knowledge about the culture and history of their diverse class.

LTL addresses all of these concerns.

Fix It-Turn It Upside Down

Remember:

- Allow selected learners to attend the workshops with you or have the professional development done with you and your entire class.
- You and your learners decide (from the ideas above or create your own) the best way to use this professional development.
- For kindergarten through second grade, identify some helpers who you want to be trained in what you are trying to learn (new strategy or information). In other words, the helpers will learn the new strategy with you. I know you are saying they are little children. Yes, they are, and they are the same little children you are expected to use the strategy with or teach the concept to. The helpers will of course help you make sure all learners

know the new strategy. Training needs to be simple enough and ready for use in the classroom.

Key: You and your selected helpers learn and teach the learners what new strategy or information you want them to learn. Don't do it to them but, rather, with them.

Benefits

You will:

- have many ears to hear, eyes to see;
- gain ideas for how to implement—your learners will think of strategies that you never would have thought of;
- create lesson plans in the training session or immediately thereafter to fit your learner needs;
- have support directly, in your classroom, all year; and
- be empowered together, directly—do it with them.

You and your learners list the benefits of this method of professional development for yourselves. Make it fit for you.

LTL Method Used to Teach Reading

L earning to Read Our Way—I created a revolutionary reading strategy that is housed in the LTL method at www.readingourway.com.

What It Is

- **learning to READ OUR WAY (ltROW)** is a revolutionary reading strategy that uses the learner's strengths, interests, culture, and history to teach reading in as little as one to two months' time.
- ltROW uses a systematic and holistic form of phonics, whole language, and critical literacy to directly teach reading, writing, speaking, thinking, listening, comprehension, and vocabulary to **groups** of struggling learners, from first grade through adulthood, in a fun, fast, easy, and empowering way.
- ltROW allows learners to **choose what and how** they learn, improving relevancy and motivation.
- ltROW provides a solid reading foundation by filling gaps so that learners function at grade level and obtain desired literacy goals.

ltROW offers so much more than a basic phonics strategy. Learners are transformed and empowered because they learn to read, understand how to learn, and change circumstances in their lives, in order to thrive in society!

We can help you change the trajectory of your life and the lives of other people!

How It Works

- ItROW's four online lessons (purchased one at a time in sequence) are taught by an instructor (a doctor in education) and viewed from the website.
- A facilitator (any person with a good fifth-grade education or above) is needed to guide **groups of learners** through the four lessons.
- The instructor and facilitator serve as *guides* on the *side*, not *sages* on the *stage*. The instructor provides the predetermined concepts and skills to be taught, and **the learners bring the lessons to life** by determining **their best way to learn** and best curricula that extend and reinforce their learning, becoming self-directed and independent learners.
- Learners work in **groups,** helping each other learn, constructing meaning, tackling social injustices, exercising choice in topics that interest them.
- Learners learn at their own rate and embrace their diverse intelligences. They become aware of their learning strengths and are able to transfer this knowledge to other learning environments.
- Learners **read a lot,** from a wide range of texts,

which increases vocabulary and comprehension quickly.

◆ Learners read texts critically, in an active, reflective manner, to better understand whose truth is being privileged, inequalities, and injustices in human relationships. They take action to make change through their reading and writing assignments and projects.

◆ One lesson, with six to eight concepts, can be learned in as little as one or two weeks when learners are engaged at least two to three hours daily, plus two or more hours of independent reading.

Who Benefits

◆ Struggling readers who are below grade level, adults, receivers of special education, and second-language learners.

◆ Learners who have not received prereading development at home and are not presently supported at home with reading development.

◆ Divergent, creative thinkers and learners with strong verbal and interpersonal skills.

◆ Learners whose knowledge and skills do not dovetail with what is needed in school to be successful.

◆ Those of whom low expectations are held and

whose history and culture are not embraced in the traditional learning environment.

◆ Teachers who need professional development in the implementation of effective and innovative instructional strategies—liberating teaching and learning.

◆ Schools, and others, with little money, a low literacy rate, and a large number of people to educate quickly and easily.

Why It Works

◆ Learners are cared for and held to high expectations—strong **affective** features.

◆ Learning is relevant. They **choose what** and **how** to learn.

◆ What is learned empowers them to make their lives better.

◆ It is student centered—learners' history and culture, interests, unique styles, needs, and intelligences are embraced and used to increase learning.

◆ Learners receive a strong reading foundation integrating phonics, whole language, and social justice. Comprehension is evidenced through real-life application.

◆ Learners teach each other, making learning faster and more fun and retention greater.

- LtROW integrates elements from successful instructional strategies (cooperative learning, differential learning, multiple intelligences, cultural learning styles, and high expectations) into the model of liberating teaching and learning.
- LtROW has helped many to read effectively in as little as two to three months, making one or two grade level gains very quickly! www.readingourway.com.

WHAT EFFECTIVE TEACHERS HAVE SAID ABOUT TEACHING AND LEARNING

I conducted an investigation with six "effective" middle school teachers in the Bay Area who taught in an ethnically diverse community. We defined "effective" as those who showed success in working with African American students. Middle school administrators were contacted and asked to refer their teachers who were "effective" in working with AA learners.

Teachers (people who would normally be considered objects of the investigation) and I were coinvestigators. That is the participatory research model. As a result of this investigation, teachers gained new knowledge and are now empowered to make changes in their own reality.

You will see after reading the dialogues and teacher responses how LTL is a natural outgrowth of the findings.

I wanted to know:

◆ the practices and behaviors of middle school teachers who were "effective" in teaching African American students;
◆ whether teachers are informed about African American students' culture and how it affects education.

Seven questions were used to gain information:

1. How would you describe your culture?
2. How would you describe the culture of African American students?
3. Describe the formal or informal training experiences specific to cross-cultural understanding you have had.
4. Tell me about your teaching experience working with African American students and some strategies you have utilized to enhance communications and interactions with these students.
5. What aspects of African American culture are considered when designing and delivering instruction?

6. Describe your ideal classroom and tell how it supports the culture of African American students.

7. If you were going to design an optimum culturally responsive teacher training program, what would it contain?

The general conclusion reached from the results of the investigation is the following:

◆ Teachers have limited knowledge of their own and their students' implicit culture (behaviors, beliefs, values, attitudes, worldview, language, and learning style, among others), while having a better understanding of students' explicit culture (food, clothing, shelter, music, among others).

◆ Teachers have limited awareness of how culture influences learning. Their instructional planning is not consciously guided by the experiences and needs of African American students.

This is why LTL is, again, so important and powerful. If the teacher doesn't know the child, the child informs the teacher when s/he is given choice in planning or teaching. Learners will choose to work from their strengths and interests. You know, teachers, we choose most often to teach our interest in subject matter and definitely deliver instruction using strategies that support our strengths. Liberate the learner to show you what they like and therefore SOAR!

Because teachers are educated in an educational system that does not value African American students' culture, they receive little positive information. If you do not extend your own learning in this regard, you bring to the classroom stereotypic views and a basic disregard for who the learner is.

I will share portions of the teachers' responses to the following questions. (These questions were left in the order they existed in the original questionnaire, hence the numbering shown in the responses below.)

1. How would you describe the culture of African American students?
2. Tell me some strategies you have utilized to enhance communications and interactions with African America students.
3. What aspects of African American culture are considered when designing and delivering instruction?
4. Describe your ideal classroom and tell how it supports the culture of African American students.

Profiles of the Participants, Followed by Responses to Selected Questions

Teachers and learners, read these conversations with the participants and glean your own insights. Use what you can. These teachers were interviewed before I created LTL. You may gain some good ideas for implementing LTL. Both of you, learner and teacher, as you read, think about how the actions of teacher as planner could have been far more enhanced had the brilliance and intelligence of the learners been unleashed and allowed to plan with the teacher.

Here we go!

A general description of each of the six participants is provided so that their critical reflections can be enriched by their personal portraits. Each participant eagerly and trustingly shared their thoughts, often after deep reflection. Teachers changed their real names.

Patricia Brown

Pat, as she is called, is a middle-aged European American woman, teaching seventh and eighth grade language arts and social studies.

2. How would you describe the culture of African American students?

(Pat feels that even though they want to achieve, some students don't have the motivation to succeed in educational situations, but they have the ability, and they are praised for their abilities.)

"Some African American students who have been put in Gifted and Talented Education GATE classes seem to turn off. I think there is a stigma attached to being in the gifted class. Parents have a strong desire for students to learn. American education is white-culture and upper-middle-class oriented, and their [African American students'] culture is lost."

3. Tell me some strategies you have utilized to enhance communications and interactions with these students.

"I get to know students individually, talk a lot, serve as a counselor, and structure the class in heterogeneous groups because it is supposed to be good for African American students. Heterogeneous grouping creates equal status among all students."

Finally, she stressed meaning-centered curriculum (we talked about math concepts and nutrition that would be meaningful in everyday situations).

Pat remembers an African American girl, Angel, who

was very strong and whom she admired a lot. Pat said, "She had that drive. She had a strong mother, and it was the mother who encouraged her."

"Angel was determined that she was not going to let me have a say in anything. She was going to be in charge. And you know, I maintained my standards. I didn't deviate, but she would question everything. This one day we were discussing myths and legends about the Greeks and the Romans and she raised her hand from the back of the room and said, 'Just tell me where do myths leave off and truth begin?' It just blew me away. I said, 'Angel, I am not sure of that answer. I'll have to think about it more and talk about it later.' We did research together and begin to make a personal connection."

Pat thought when Angel left that school that she would never see her again, because Pat was so strict, but Angel popped in to see her often. When Pat asked Angel why she came by so often, Angel replied, "You were honest with me."

4. What aspects of African American culture are considered when designing and delivering instruction?
Pat reflected a bit and thought. "I don't know: maybe letting them be themselves, giving opportunities to talk

about their own lifestyles and things that are going on in their lives and that they are interested in."

Pat believes that tapping into their abilities and interest decreased behavior problems.

"I also found that there were lots of students who were capable of doing more things than they were given credit for. I let them do their own self-assessments, so they are always aware of what and how much they are learning.

"My salvation is to get to know them individually. I work with them in groups, and we talk about working together. Your role becomes one of a counselor and facilitator. I had a lot of opportunities to work with kids individually and also in groups, and we talked a lot. They would come in at lunchtime and we would chat."

Pat remembers after the semester was over, kids were much happier about where they were. She also remembers the students trying to teach her to talk like them.

Pat said she told them, "I would practice, but I can't talk the way you do because I am not you. What I enjoyed most about them was that they were expressing exactly who they are."

Pat talked about her training in and the use of cooperative learning in her classroom, because of its effectiveness with African American and Latino students. The benefits include a stimulation of more complex cognitive meanings. Children developed their own voices, began to recognize the voices of others, and recognized the similarities and differences of views.

"The more I use the strategy of cooperative learning, the more I believe that all students have abilities. Cooperative learning really does give all students a chance to show their abilities and contribute in a meaningful way to the class."

5. Describe your ideal classroom and tell how it supports the culture of African American students.
Pat describes a supportive and collaborative classroom around her, which exemplifies the philosophy that all students have ability and it is up to the teacher to bring it out.

"My ideal classroom will be self-learning—all kids would have the opportunity to learn and share their learning and abilities with others. They would learn about each other's culture. Everyone would be learning from everybody else."

Diane Harvey

Diane is an African American woman who is beginning her twenty-fifth year of employment, of which seven years were spent teaching elementary school. The rest have been spent teaching middle school, sixth- and seventh-grade social studies.

2. How would you describe the culture of African American students?

Diane describes African American students' culture as being rich, but says it has been demeaned a lot and has not been addressed properly. "They (students) don't know who they are, don't know their background, and they have been misrepresented. Their culture hasn't been honestly printed in the textbooks. It's been very biased and very colonial."

Diane expresses delight and hope in reversing past practices in what she calls "the voluminous amount of writings out on the market by people from our own culture. We are writing about our own history. Now you don't get this Eurocentric attitude, but you're getting the culture itself in its fairness and what it needs to say to us."

3. Tell me about some strategies you have utilized to

enhance communications and interactions with African American students.

Diane is the only Black teacher on the staff, and she has very few African American students. There are not many in her school. Diane serves as a role model, acts as a liaison between students and teachers, and helps to clarify the use of English for some students from the Caribbean. Diane has created student assistance programs—for example, an adopt-a-student-program for students who have the potential of falling between the cracks and the peer-helping program, where students pair with a partner to receive support socially and academically.

Diane later added, "I share my own experiences with students to personalize the curriculum or situation."

4. What aspects of African American culture are considered when designing and delivering instruction?
Diane believes that there is no such thing as can't, so she designs lessons for success. She said, "I support them in tackling a bit of their work at a time. We throw a lot of stuff at kids and expect the kids to be successful; it's just too much for them to absorb.

"So, for me, when I was taught my ABCs back at home, I could remember how we were taught to go at it methodically and a bit at a time. My parents and teachers always emphasized, if you can't get it all, get a little bit, but try to get as much as you can get out of it, and this is what I like to do. Even if it takes me a week to get something finished, it doesn't matter to me."

Diane describes an example of a project she has implemented over the years. The project involves helping kids to really develop an attitude of caring for one another and stressing that everyone should get to know about each other's culture.

"My theme is 'Share the Spirit of Diversity,' and those kids came out 'slammin'. We studied all the cultures. First, I took a census of all the cultures that I had in the three classes of sixth graders. Then, we decided to deal with language, foods, sports, education, and government of origin (student or parents)."

"Students see how the present and past cultures interrelate. They understand that, 'Hey, I don't have to give up my culture.' Students went to different booths, where student docents carry them through each culture."

"So, now, the other teachers and Parent Teacher Association PTA are doing the activity. It is one of the greatest experiences that the school has ever had in the community. Student accountability is built in through graded activities and follow-up assignments."

5. Describe your ideal classroom and tell how it supports the culture of African American students.
Diane explains that she would want a larger population of African American students in her class. Students would be caring for one another. There would be unity among them. They would know and respect each other's culture.

Bob Karl

Bob, a European American male, is entering his fourth year of teaching. He teaches physical education, student government (a leadership class), and science. Bob adds, "I do a lot of coaching after school as well."

2. How would you describe the culture of African American students?
Bob describes culture in explicit terms. He recalls the school's International Thanksgiving Day, when he sees some African American students participating in the school celebrations with foods and wearing African attire.

3. Tell me about some strategies you have utilized to enhance communications and interactions with these students.
"Strategies I use are get to know the person, know that environmental issues create problems for students."

Bob remembers one of his very first experiences: "I had a very hard core African American girl who had a lot of anger and a lot of real frustration. When I had her for physical education, I really wanted her to do something for the basketball team because she was a really good athlete. I thought I could get to her that way, since I was a PE teacher focusing on athletics and being physical.

"However, she just had a number of things going on in her life that would not allow her to participate to her fullest. She ended up getting kicked off the team for incidents that occurred. I wondered why couldn't she just have a positive attitude. Then you do a little more research and find out who the person goes home to every night and what their environment is like."

Bob feels that because he teaches PE, he is able to reach students who may be having problems in academic areas.

He recounts some success stories: "I have had some students, one in particular who moved earlier this year, who was always pretty pleasant to me in my PE class, whereas I have heard nothing but horror stories from the other teachers who had him at a desk (classroom)."

"My student body president this year was African American, and she had moments of brilliance. She was also on the basketball team. I had some other African American students who helped me out with after-school training programs."

4. What aspects of African American culture are considered when designing and delivering instruction?
Bob thought that the curriculum he uses has no cultural base, but he includes African American role models—very popular African American athletes—whenever possible.

5. Describe your ideal classroom and tell how it supports the culture of African American students.
Bob's PE classes are very large. The number-one concern was to have fewer than forty-five students to ensure that each student experiences success and is recognized for his/her achievement. There would be a wide variety of outcomes, and peer coaching would be one.

Teresa Hughes

Teresa, an African American woman, has completed twenty-five years teaching, all of which have been at the middle level. She has taught at all levels, but predominately in the seventh grade.

2. How would you describe the culture of African American students?

Teresa finds that the difference she notices between now and years ago in what students know about their culture is a little upsetting. Students knew more in the past about who they were and who they could be. They knew more about their culture than now. "We have let our guard down and have awakened to find that students don't know who they are—African American youngsters."

3. Tell me about some strategies you have utilized to enhance communications and interactions with these students.

"I get to know students, engage in one-on-one conversations with them. Remain neutral in conflict and assure them that we will talk about it later, because students think teachers are not fair. Some teachers show less tolerance for African American students than others. But just in casual observations, and what I hear through conversations, I do think some of my fellow Anglo teachers jump the gun and don't take that other step that I see them take with other kids.

"It is something hard to put your finger on. I think, sometimes, they are truly unaware of it. Nevertheless, students' claims of unfair treatment are real."

Teresa shared how she addresses student claims of unfair treatment. "I think you have to follow the claim of unfairness with a conversation by themselves to identify exactly what it is that they think is unfair. I'm finding that I have to do that because I can't assume I know what they mean. I find out that what they mean and what I thought they meant have nothing whatsoever to do with each other."

4. What aspects of African American culture are considered when designing and delivering instruction?
Teresa said she is aware of the posters, books, projects, and vignettes that reflect contributions of African Americans. She personalizes the curriculum with discussion opportunities on issues—such as health, family life, and racism—that surface through current events.

Part of personalizing the lesson that Teresa does, when discussing the circulatory system, is sharing with her class that Dr. Charles Drew was her father's cousin.

At her school, the vignettes are created and announced over the school intercom during Black History Month, and students respond to the question "Did you know?" a particular fact about African Americans.

It has become an important activity at the school, and students expect her to have her posters and other learning aids up to assist them in answering the questions. She also has posters of astronauts, inventions, and medical research.

Except for these materials and activities, Teresa said she does not consciously do anything else to consider African American students' culture when delivering instruction.

5. Describe your ideal classroom and tell how it supports the culture of African American students.
Teresa feels that she would want culturally sensitive curriculum in her science class. She would have a number of visuals, student projects, posters reflecting the contributions of African Americans and/or Hispanics and other groups. Group and individual learning would take place (cooperative learning). Additional space is needed for group learning arrangements.

Teresa voiced her dissatisfaction with all the science textbooks which she has seen, so she would like money to buy classroom resources, especially books that are inclusive of all cultures.

Elise Mwalimi

Elise, an African American woman, describes herself as the student who would not conform and was always in trouble. Because of that, she identifies with many of her middle school students. Eight of her eleven years teaching have been in middle school. Elise served this year as a coordinator and coach for the Algebra Project, assisting teachers in the implementation of the math program in their classrooms.

2. How would you describe the culture of African American students?

Elise spoke about African American students' culture with a heavy emphasis on rhythm and energy. "It is rhythmic, energetic, movement, musical (humming), need for fairness, and sincerity."

"It is, I want to learn everything, and I am willing to allow you to teach me if I believe that you really want to teach me.

"We keep a rhythm. Rhythm in the way we learn. If the rhythm gets out of control (as manifested in misbehaviors), then the rhythm is off."

Movement and energy are often what get our children in trouble in school because they are misperceived as hyperactivity, but movement, as Elise says, is what everyone does.

"I don't know very many people who can actually sit and have nothing moving. Their hearts are beating. I mean, something has got to move."

Elise's view is consistent with research conducted by Boykin (1978), when he identifies nine interrelated dimensions of the African American experience. The third dimension is movement—an emphasis on rhythm, music, and dance. Irvine (1991) also supports Elise's view when she observes that "rhythm" is the essential word that Pasteur and Toldson (1982) use to characterize African American culture. They refer to this concept as the "basic ingredient of Black people's expressiveness."

Elise speaks further on what breaks the rhythm of African American students. "Behavior is universal. People behave based on how they are treated. If they are mistreated, they will behave in a way to show that they don't like what is being done to them. Students are disrespected by the adults in their environment, especially the way they are talked to."

3. Tell me some strategies you have utilized to enhance communications and interactions with these students. Elise explained strategies she uses:

"We sit and talk—round-table discussions. We discuss what affects them and determine what we need to start the day. We look at what's happening or bothering them and what they are thinking about. We talk about the type of things we want to learn in the class and how do we want to learn them. I create a safe climate for discussion."

Although all the participants spoke about using the strategy of talking to their students, Elise spoke most about how to talk to students. She speaks to students with lots of respect—she talks to them and not at them. She also stresses the importance of listening and allowing students to say what they want (of course, what they say must be respectful).

She explained: "If you actually look at them and invite their responses—I mean really, really invite it and question or respond as if you are really listening to them. For example, the listener could say, 'I didn't realize that you were thinking that way.' Then the student knows you are really listening to them and will participate more in class conversations and discussions."

Elise commented on other strategies she uses with great success: "I instituted the court system, which creates opportunities for fairness to prevail using their own knowledge to solve their own problems."

The court system which Elise instituted grew out of a need to give students alternative ways to resolve their issues without fighting.

Students create a court-of-law system to determine the fairness or unfairness of their classmates' and teacher's behavior. The entire court is designed and manned by the students. The teacher has no more power than any student.

Elise comments that "students take on very responsible roles and everybody abides by the decisions that are made. It's just a beautiful thing to watch. Their peers are truly their peers, and they're not like these people who have nothing to do with them. These are their classmates who know the truth. The jury are actually the rest of the classmates.

"When instituting a court system, the teacher has to give up some of the perceived power in the classroom. I gain more power. I don't give up the power. I just share the power. When I share the power, I'm looked at as a person that is fair. So, that gives me more power. When I am out on the yard with other kids, they know that I am a fair person. So, they will listen. They already know that I don't plan to take control over them.

"So, I am viewed as a different power force than the one who deals out punishment. They understand that it's more like, 'She's trying to make us come to an agreement or get an understanding here. She's going to talk to us.'"

This practice is consistent with Hilliard's (1985) description of African American cultural style, when he explains that African American people have a keen sense of justice and are quick to analyze and perceive injustice.

This descriptor helps to explain why students in Elise's class are able to design and conduct the court system with such proficiency.

On the Algebra Project, Elise explains it as a way to start students off, in the teaching of a concept, with shared/common experiences where everybody is on the same playing field. The process requires students to draw pictures of what they experience, write about it in their own words, discuss it, then make the abstract representations. She adds, "I really try to use it as a way of helping African American students and other students of color to learn".

Elise also gives her students a chance to teach the class; usually the last month of school is the time to teach: "They have to pick something they had learned and really enjoyed through the year. They must bring the material and teaching aids. They really teach, and I sit down and I learn too. I'm never out of the class. I don't want to sound like I don't come down on kids when they get out of control, because I do. But there are more times when it's just a pleasant place to be than it is unpleasant.

"People would come to my class and say it was like being at home. You could actually just sit down and have people moving and working."

4. What aspects of African American culture are considered when designing and delivering instruction?
Elise uses the Algebra Project curriculum, designed and popularized by Bob Moses. It is being implemented in schools across the nation with large African American student populations. It is a math curriculum process that stresses the use of students' prior knowledge and shared experiences within a common environment. It moves from the concrete to the abstract meaning.

Elise explained the technique: "The Algebra Project Curriculum process is where we start with something physical which represents a shared experience. We draw pictures of the experience. Write about the experience in our own words and talk about the symbolic representations for algebra. This process supports the movement and rhythm of African American students and respects who you are and what you know."

"I might add, the Algebra Project allows learners to move from the concrete to the abstract."

5. Describe your ideal classroom and tell how it supports the culture of African American students.
Elise would design an affective classroom with the cognitive attached. Her ideal classroom reflects her desire for students to be involved, have choices, and expend energy while engaging in rigorous academic pursuits.

She says, "Just give me and my sixth graders a skeleton of what is important to learn, and we will do the rest. The students would determine what, where, when, and how much we would learn. Students will have their assignments and take responsibility for completing them. Students will work individually and in groups."

"In the classroom environment, you would see people moving about, asking questions, everybody helping each other, talking, laughing, telling jokes, while work is being done. The teacher and students are sharing the roles of teacher and coach."

Florence Fan

Florence, an African American woman, is entering her last year of service before retirement. She has taught for many years, and six of those years have been in middle schools. She has served in other capacities in schools, as program coordinator and teacher trainer of storytelling and effective language-arts strategies.

2. How would you describe the culture of African American students?

The indicators Florence used to describe her own culture were the same ones used when she was asked to describe the culture of African American students.

"In some ways, I would describe their culture as a minority. As one which the students should be taught to be proud of."

When Florence was asked to define culture, her description was much broader and more characteristic of implicit elements.

"I would define culture as something that's handed down from people in your family. What you are taught at home (my mom and grandmother were in the home) at a very early age. It's about who you are and what you are. Who you can be and what you can do. So, it's something that's learned. And it changes. Individuals change it."

This view is consistent with Levine (1977) that culture is not a fixed condition, but a process: the product of interaction between the past and present.

3. Tell me about some strategies you have utilized to enhance communications and interactions with these students.

Florence often stressed that she does not separate strategies based on cultural group needs.

"I never had just an African American class. I don't separate. I teach with a whole class focus. I am not aware of specific strategies for African American students. Some of the strategies I've used to include all students, but namely to pull in the African American students, include research on various cultures, use of many visuals, I have them write poetry and stories, and I do lots of storytelling."

Upon further reflection, Florence mentioned, "There are many times when I talk, especially to African American students when they are not achieving. I express how important it is for them to do their homework and to do the best that they can. As a minority group, we have it harder. But I really don't think about it."

When asked if she thought it might be something that warrants some thought, she thought that it did and added, reiterating, "I talk to kids about life and about the difficulties of life. Being an African American myself, I talk about how hard it is for them in the world. I try to make them aware of the importance of them giving more time for their studies."

4. What aspects of African American culture are considered when designing and delivering instruction? Florence's initial reflection on this question produced this reply:

"I don't. If I were teaching Black Studies or just African American kids, then maybe I would." She added, "I talk to African American students and encourage them and express how important it is to do their best, to achieve, and to do their homework. As a minority group, we have it harder."

The views are consistent with research of scholars who say that many children who believe they are not liked by their teachers do not like themselves or school. These students feel isolated, discouraged, and eventually fail academically. They are more teacher dependent and are more likely to hold the teacher in high esteem.

5. Describe your ideal classroom and tell how it supports the culture of African American students. Florence's ideal classroom reflects her strong background and interest in literature.

"There would be lots of books and pictures of African Americans, lists of achievements that African Americans have made. I feel as a teacher, I shouldn't separate the African American culture from any other culture. I try to integrate boys and girls from all cultures. The classroom would provide a comfortable atmosphere for learning."

All teachers connected to the culture of the learners, some without knowing it. As you can see, the affective domain that we talked about earlier was the area the teachers tapped into most. They did so by showing that they cared, talking and listening to learners, allowing them to express themselves, and tapping into their hard/surface culture. A couple of teachers tapped into some of the soft/hidden culture.

Remember the saying, "People don't care how much you know, until they know how much you care." Theodore Roosevelt.

What Do Culturally Supportive Teachers Do?

It cannot be overstated how important teachers' attitude, beliefs, and expectations are for learners' academic success. Culturally supportive teaching is a way of teaching that allows teachers and learners to use history and culture as the foundation for curriculum and instruction, thus empowering students intellectually, socially, emotionally.

Culturally supportive teachers stress the affect; even if they don't know students' culture, they talk, and show they care by listening and helping them to solve their problems. Very important.

The importance of teachers in the lives of their students is not to be minimized. Teachers influence students' achievement and their cognitive development, but they influence self-concept and attitudes as well.

In the words of one of the participants, Elise, "We want the best type of teaching to happen for all students. And if it works for students of color, then more than likely it will work for all students." I agree.

Lots of research shows the relationship between a child's cultural environment and his or her school success. Check them out if you desire: Du Bois (1969), Ogbu (1978), Irvine (1991), Shade (1993).

Teachers are not receiving enough, if any, professional development to address the ways that culture influences learning and students' behavior in the classroom. That is why LTL is so important because it allows teacher and students to learn students' culture in real time. This does not prevent you from learning about students' culture in other ways.

Indeed, some of you are impacting AA students in positive ways. AA students are able to identify such teacher attributes. A young Black man discussing a former teacher, "good teacher," with a group of friends: "We had fun in her class, but she was mean.

I can remember she used to say, 'Tell me what's in the story, Wayne.' She pushed. She used to get on me and push me to know. She made us learn. We had to get in the books." It is impossible to create a model for the good teacher without taking issues of culture into consideration.

Wayne speaks to the cultural value of responsibility and high expectations—and most of all the sense of caring that the teacher's behavior demonstrates. These are concepts in the affective domain of education, where most of African Americans' cultural characteristics fall.

PARTICIPANTS' REFLECTIONS ON THE METHODOLOGY

Participatory research methodology was a welcomed process to use to dialogue with the participants. The excitement, expectation, and anxiety of both researcher and participants produced a harmonized energy which contributed to a powerful experience.

Participants shared ways in which they were moved toward continued reflection after our dialogue.

Diane called me on the phone immediately after her trip to South America and stated: "Please add this to the effective strategies I use with my students. I always share my own personal experiences with them. This is a neat study. I thought of this on a bus ride in Peru."

Diane further stated, "This process of sharing strategies is quite enriching and enlightening. Things that I have been concerned with, and I am so happy that somebody is pursuing them. It has been very empowering because there were things that I never thought about, some issues that I never thought about dealing with or attempting to deal with, for that matter, because I felt they were irrelevant and thought it was a lost cause. I'm so happy that this opportunity came for me to really unearth them again and to give expression so they can become Bible to the investigator and her work."

Pat returned to our final meeting announcing:

"I met over the summer with another middle school teacher to plan a unit on Africa and wanted to present an accurate picture of the people of Africa and the part Europeans have played in Africa's history. I want you to review the unit before I teach it."

She shared her reflections on the process. "This experience has been one that I will never forget. It has certainly helped me understand more about the African American culture. It has also helped me understand more about the needs that I have in working with the students in the classroom. I'm really understanding more and more through this experience that the prejudice that we have is because of the implicit culture of the African American."

"So, what I want the kids to understand is more of the implicit culture. I'm looking forward to really bringing a lot more understanding to the students that I teach."

Elise expressed at the end of our dialogue, "This is like therapy." Florence stated, "This is sort of fun." It was moments like these that crystallized the impact of such a process.

We used this opportunity not only to get to know each other better but also to learn from each other. "Both were changed." We improved and enriched our own lives and engaged in the commitment to try to do the same for African American students.

In this investigation, teachers participated in generating the solutions themselves, not me, the investigator. Likewise, LTL engages learners and teachers in generating ideas about best practices for their classrooms. As they do, curriculum and instruction are being informed by the personal needs, interests, and cultural perspectives of the learner and teacher. This is easy and saves major time for the teacher—no guess work. This kind of teacher/learner planning produces powerful experiences.

Learners' Voices on Curriculum-Giving Voice to Students

S tudent curriculum choices vs. teacher choices. This is an example of how different curriculum choices made by learners could be from those made by others. These learner choices were only able to be implemented for a short time, but learners were ready to continue with the lessons.

So, just think how motivated and excited learners will be when, every day and every lesson, they are given choices.

Relevant Curriculum and Instruction

Effective teachers realize that students come to school with a wealth of information and skills and find ways to utilize them. On the other hand, other teachers do not utilize the skills and information because they do not dovetail with the school curriculum. So, students' knowledge and skills are devalued. Therefore, the student is devalued. Freire (1973) states that the learner is not an empty vessel to be filled by the teacher, nor an object of education.

I engaged a seventh-grade English class (twenty-one boys and seven girls, all African Americans) in a process to collaboratively develop relevant curriculum. I posed the following question to be answered.

Question: In what ways will students' behaviors be influenced when students are given the opportunity to engage in a learning experience based on their interest and supportive of their culture?

Students were asked to submit written responses to the following questions:

What question do you want to have answered? What do you want to learn more about?

A process which includes students in the development of curriculum can use student-generated questions as a guide for ensuring that their concerns are being addressed (creating curriculum relevancy) and for giving them ownership in the learning process.

Their responses were compiled and returned to them. From this, three priority themes emerged:

- ◆ Sex education,
- ◆ Racism, and
- ◆ Child–parent relationships.

We chose the number-one priority—sex education.

Students submitted questions reflecting what they wanted to know about sex education. Their questions ranged from specific concerns about sexual intercourse and sexually transmitted diseases, to why girls and boys like each other. Those specific questions were compiled to form curriculum, which was used to teach a small unit on sex education.

The class was taught once a week for eleven weeks with culturally supportive instructional strategies such as cooperative learning, discussions, poetry writing and reading, and a Dear Abby format, which allowed students to pose problems anonymously and have them discussed and have resolutions offered.

The findings indicated that, when students collaborated in the development of curriculum which used culturally supported instructional strategies, students' curriculum needs and interests in sex education were very different from the California State–prescribed sex education curriculum. Students expressed excitement and motivation—and showed retention.

They expressed excitement about being given the opportunity to have their concerns addressed. They constantly asked whether those questions were "really" going to be answered. They liked the idea that they were going to actually have their questions and concerns addressed in the classroom. Motivation and retention were high.

Motivation: during the classes, they asked questions, eagerly participated in discussions, and offered, for the most part, thoughtful solutions to problems posed by their peers.

Retention: students would remember most of what we discussed from one week to the next, when, often, most information is forgotten one day to the next. For example, students remembered responses to the problem-posing situations which had been done 2–3 weeks earlier and reminded us that violence had come up and was a theme for a subsequent unit. This is an example of what can happen when students' knowledge is valued and their needs are being met. They, like everyone else, want to be heard, to be validated, and to learn what they need in order to be better human beings who contribute to and thrive in society.

Effective teachers in this investigation acknowledge their students and value what they bring to school. The teachers spent time talking with students to learn of their experiences and interests and attempted to integrate these into the curriculum. Teachers expressed dissatisfaction with current textbooks and other teaching materials which give meager attention to African American students' history and culture.

Diane spoke about being tired of learning about White people's culture, because it has no relevance to her life, or to the life of her students. Banks and Banks (1993) say that students learn best and are more highly motivated when the school curriculum reflects their cultures, experiences, and perspectives.

LTL frees learners to coplan and coteach and include learners' choices and interests into daily lessons as opposed to sporadic episodes. LTL advocates for radical classroom restructuring without any added time and little money. Change has come to American classrooms.

CONCLUSIONS FROM THE EFFECTIVE TEACHER INVESTIGATION

What we learned from this investigation became another reason to create LTL. What we learned suggests that the foundation for success and the prerequisite for African American student achievement appear to be committed, caring (taking time to get to know each student), dedicated, well-trained teachers who believe that all students can learn and who will go the extra mile in working with African American students to ensure their success.

This supportive relationship between teacher and student is a fundamental necessity from which all other solutions and interventions emerge. Because the educational system was not designed for African Americans, Elise uses an analogy to explain what happens when some African American students enter this foreign (school) setting.

"It's like walking into someone's house (school), and you're like their foster child. This house is not yours. Everything is in its place already. Because it does not belong to you, you don't have any buy-in, you are just a visitor there and feel you are not going to be there long."

To extend Elise's analogy, the people (educators) of the house expect you to come in and adapt to their ways without ever taking time to learn anything about your ways—you become invisible.

If we are to ever escape the racism and oppression that continue to impair our natural development, we must think seriously of developing and controlling our own models for educational change.

This must be our mission: to ensure that our African American children not only survive but rise to the heights they are capable of achieving. When we lift them, we lift others. This is another reason why I created Liberating Teaching and Learning. It's been a long time coming, but change has come to American classrooms.

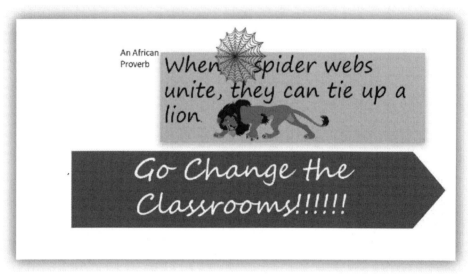

Actions to Take

Visit the website www.readingourway.com to:

- Share your progress, after reading the book and using LTL;
- Schedule a combined teacher and learner training in the Liberating Teaching and Learning (LTL) strategy, or access the "Learning to Read Our Way" classes and teach learners to read.

Form Book Clubs

References (Look up These Authors' "You Tubes")

Adair, Alvis. 1984. *Desegregation: The Illusion of Black Progress.* New York: University Press of America.

Armstrong, Thomas. 1987. *In Their Own Way.* New York: Penguin Publishing Group, 1ˢᵗ edition.

Banks, James, and Cherry Banks. 1993. *Multicultural Education: Issues and Perspectives.* Needham, MA: Allyn and Bacon.

Bloom, Benjamin. 1977. Human Characteristics and School Learning. Phi Delta Kappa International, Bloomington, IN

Boykin, A. Wade. 1978. *Psychological Behavioral Verve in Academic Task Performance: Pre-Theoretical Considerations. Journal of Negro Ed,* 47 (Winter): 343–54.

Boykin, A. Wade, and Brenda Allen. 1992. "African American Children and the Educational Process: Alleviating Cultural Discontinuity through Prescriptive Pedagogy." *School Psychology Review,* 21 (4): 586–596.

Boykins, A. Wade. 1986. The Triple Quandary and Schooling of Afro- American Children. Lawrence Erlbaum Associates Publishers, Mahwah, NJ

Brandt, Godfrey. 1986. *The Realization of Anti-Racist Teaching.* London: Taylor and Francis.

The Council of Interracial Books for Children Inc. (CIBC) "The Bulletin, The Fact Sheet on Institutional Racism." (social justice books, films, lessons).

Decker, Barbara. 1983. Cultural Diversity, Another Element to Recognize in Learning Styles. NASSPBulletin . #67.

DuBois, W.E.B. 1969. The Souls of Black Folk. Nal Penguin Inc. Publishers. New York, NY

Freire, Paulo. 1973. *Education for Critical Consciousness.* New York: Continuum.

Freire, Paulo, and Ira Shor. 1987. *A Pedagogy for Liberation: Dialogues on Transforming Education.* New York: Bergin and Garvey Publishers.

Freire, Paulo. 1973. Education for Critical Consciousness. Continuum. New York, NY

Goodlad, John. 1983. A Place Called School: Prospects for the Future (A Study of Schooling in the United States). McGraw- Hill, New York, NY

Hale-Benson, Janice. 1987. *Black Children: Their Roots, Culture, and Learning Styles.* Provo, UT: Brigham Young University Press.

Hilliard, Asa. 1985. "Teachers and Cultural Styles in a Pluralistic Society." National Education Association.

Irvine, Jacqueline. 1991. Black Students and School Failure. Greenwood Press, Inc. Westport, CT

Kochman, Thomas. 1981. *Black and White Styles in Conflict.* Chicago: University of Chicago Press.

Levine, Lawrence. 1977. Black Consciousness. Oxford University Press. New York, NY

Martinez Smith, Elizabeth. 1988. "Racism: It Is Always There" (article from speech given at the American Library Association Conference).

Mimi, A. 1967. The Colonizer and Colonized. Beacon Press, Boston, MA

Nobles, Wade. 1990. "Understanding African American

Culture: A Teacher's Guide." Unpublished manuscript, San Francisco State University, San Francisco.

Nobles, Wade. 1991. "The Infusion of African American Content: A Question of Content and Intent." Unpublished manuscript, San Francisco State University, San Francisco.

Ogbu, John. 1978. Minority Education and Caste. Academic Press. New York, NY

Pasteur, Alfred. and Tolson, Ivory. 1982. Roots of Soul: The Psychology of Black Expressiveness. Anchor Press Double Day. New York, NY

The Pew Research Center. "American Public School Teachers Are Far Less Racially and Ethnically Diverse Than Their Students." U.S. Department of Education, National Center for Education Statistics.

Shade, Barbara and New, Clara. 1993. Cultural Influences on Learning: Teaching Implications. Allyn and Bacon. Boston, MA

Woodson, Carter. 1933. *Mis-Education of the Negro.* Philadelphia, PA: Hakim Publications.

The Washington Post. "One in Five U.S. Schoolchildren Are Living below Federal Poverty Line," by Lyndsey Layton.

Recommended Books and YouTube Channels for African/African American History

The majority of these authors have YouTube presentations/discussions of their books.

LTL encourages creation of your personal bibliography

- Africa: Mother of Western Civilization (African American Heritage Series): Yosef Ben Jochannan
- "And don't call *me* a racist!": Ella Mazel
- Before The Mayflower: Lerone Bennet Jr.
- Between the World and Me: Ta Nehisi Coates
- Black Labor, White Wealth—The Search for Power and Economic Justice: Claud Anderson
- Breaking the Chains of Psychological Slavery: Na'im Akbar
- From the Browder File: Anthony T. Browder
- Hidden Figures: Margaret Lee Shetterly
- How Europe Underdeveloped Africa: Walter Rodney
- Isis Papers: Frances Cress Welsing
- Lies My Teacher Told Me—Everything Your American History Textbook Got Wrong: James Loewen
- Melanin: The Chemical Key to Black Greatness (Black Greatness Series): Carol Barnes

- Precolonial Black Africa: Cheikh Anta Diop
- Stamped from the Beginning: Ibram X Kendi
- Stolen Legacy: The Greeks Were Not the Authors of Greek Philosophy: George James
- The African Origin of Civilization: Myth or Reality: Cheikh Anta Diop
- The African World: Professor Small (view his videos and read any of his works)
- The Destruction of Black Civilization: Chancellor Williams
- The Immortal Life of Henrietta Lacks: Rebecca Skloot
- The Legacy of Malthus—The Social Costs of the New Scientific Racism: Allan Chase
- The Times Present #1619 (observing the 400th anniversary of American enslavement): Nikole Hannah-Jones
- The Mis-Education of the Negro: Carter G. Woodson
- They Came before Columbus: Ivan Van Sertima
- What They Never Taught You in History Class: Indus Khamit Kush

European American Authors/ Activists on Racism and Culture

- *Uprooting Racism: What White People Can Do to Stop Racism*: Paul Kivel
- *When Society Becomes an Addict*: Anne Scheaf
- *White Like Me: Reflections on Race from a Privileged Son*: Tim Wise
- *White Privilege: Unpacking the Invisible Knapsack*: Peggy McIntosh

Younger Readers

- *A is for Activist* by Innosanto Nargara
- *Anti-Biased Curriculum: Tools for Empowering Young Children* by Louise Denmark Parks and the ABC Task Force
- *Black Books Matter: Children's Books Celebrating Black Boys*
- *I Am Enough* by Grace Byers
- *I Love My Hair* by Natasha Anastasia Tarpley
- *Marley Diaz Gets It Done: And So Can You* by Marley Diaz
- *Melanin 'n' Me* by Beverly Crespo
- *M for Movement* by Innosanto Nargara
- *Reading Blackout:* Children's books written by African American authors
- *Reading, Writing and Rising Up: Teaching about*

Social Justice and the Power of the Written Word by Linda Christensen
- *Rethinking Our Classrooms: Teaching for Equity and Justice* by Bill Bigelow
- *Stirring Up Justice: Writing and Reading to Change the World* by Jessica Singer
- *The Conscious Kid (a list of 25 children's books celebrating Black boys)* by Moms of Black Boys United
- *When God Made You* by Matthew Paul Turner

YouTube

"The Doll Test by Kenneth and Mamie Clark—The Effects That Racism Has on Children"

"The Real Magic of Melanin: Amazing Things You Didn't Know"

ACKNOWLEDGMENTS

I had no interest in writing a book beyond my doctoral work. However, Big Sister would often ask, "When are you going to write your book?" Thanks for that little seed of inspiration. Realizing that the mounting experiences, knowledge, and skills I have gained could be transforming for teachers and students (especially African Americans, who benefit least from the present classroom structure) and had implications for the entire educational system, I had to share it. I did, and I feel purged. I know the universe will land it in the right place at the right time.

Clifford, whose spirit sustains me, didn't get to see the finished product. You listened to my complaints and would offer these encouraging words: "You can get it done." I wish you were here to share it with me.

Darryl, for being there from the beginning to the end, offering feedback on the title, design elements, layout, cover, reading and editing drafts—gracias for your invaluable help.

Bernard Cistrunk, thanks for lending your experiences to enrich this book and for your feedback on title selection.

My precious boys and girls, whose names I promised not to use, thank you (and your parents) for agreeing to offer your honest opinions, and so quickly, about how you would re-teach lessons previously taught in the classroom. Your voices bring authenticity where it counts most. Also, thanks to the "effective teachers" who participated in my doctoral work. Your insights are just as important as they were then. This Liberating Teaching and Learning strategy is the next step in advancing teachers' effectiveness.

Thanks to Jason and Vidya for lending another set of eyes that provided a thorough review of and feedback on my work and for meticulously maintaining the structure of my manuscript during the layout while adding enhancements for diverse readers. Good job. Thanks to my designer who did a good job in capturing and representing my vision for the cover.

Finally, the truth tellers and thought leaders, some of whom I sat with and others whose scholarship I devoured, have imbued me with wisdom, knowledge, insights, and inspiration that shaped my thoughts, beliefs, and behaviors, of which this book is a reflection. To these few—Carter G. Woodson, James Baldwin, Wade Nobles, Asa Hilliard, Frances Cress Welsing, A. Wade Boykin, Anita DeFrantz, John Henrik Clarke, George James, John Hope Franklin, Paulo Freire, and Cheikh Anta Diop – I offer *Liberating Teaching and Learning,* and send boundless gratitude.

Made in the USA
Columbia, SC
16 October 2021